JESUS

A NEW COVENANT

A message for *A Course in Miracles* students

WWW.JOININGINLIGHT.NET

Disclaimer

No words are true. Words can only point to Truth. This text is given for the purpose of serving the recognition of the One, and can be confirmed only in the heart of each being with the willingness to inquire within to see what is true, that Infinite Light is always here. This is the Light that lights everyone who is born before thoughts and thus words arise. Light is indescribable, immutable and unchanged by any words. This text has no purpose other than for inquiry into the nature of the Light of Divine Being, the recognition of what is far beyond words.

For more information email: join@joininginlight.net

First paperback edition December 2021

Book design by Grzegorz Japoł (book-cover.design)

ISBN 978-1-7375145-0-3 (paperback)
ISBN 978-1-7375145-1-0 (hard cover)

www.JoininginLight.net

Table of Contents

INTRODUCTION

Jesus: A New Covenant ACIM is a new means for transcending the idea of personal identity–an identity separate from God–that is the cause of all pain and suffering of the world. Jesus, as the symbol of the Light within all beings, offers a fast means to spiritual awakening through a deep look at the denials of Divinity that are hidden in the subconscious mind. This book is not for discussion of metaphysics; rather, it is for deep contemplation and for direct experience of the peace of mind and Infinite Love that is always available. All else is a denial of Light. This text, along with Light Circles to look at the denials of the Light of Truth, is a means to quickly recognize the Light within and to see that there is only Light–Infinite Light–that is unlimited by any idea of this world. While the text refers to the teachings of *A Course in Miracles*, no experience is needed with the Course, as all beings are Light Beings and thus can recognize and celebrate the Light within. This is a powerful non-dual path that is both a fast and practical means to see that what is granted–perfect peace, health and happiness, everything given by Infinite Love–is always available, unless it is denied through the desire to experience the thought system of the ego.

About Joining in Light

Joining in Light is a symbol for coming together as Light Beings to honor the Light within; when two or more are gathered in His name there is Love. This is a reminder that all beings are Light Beings and can come together to celebrate this Light to see that darkness, the idea of suffering and pain, is an idea that cannot co-exist with the Light of Truth. It is a reminder to focus on Light within and to place all thoughts, feelings and emotions in the Light with willingness to see what is true. The Holy Spirit and Jesus are symbols of this Light, the Light that lights everyone who is born. In this Light the Voice for God can be heard–the inner voice of Divine Nature–that provides guidance for the way back to the recognition that Divine Light is all there is. This is the inner peace and joy that surpasses understanding that is pointed to in all mystical spiritual traditions. Thus, *Jesus: A New Covenant ACIM* is a simple and direct non-dual path to spiritual awakening–recognition of Divinity–and because of the simplicity suitable for beings of all backgrounds and ages.

The symbols of Joining in Light in the form of *Light Circles* and *Jesus: A New Covenant ACIM* were extended to Cay Villars in mystical visions and conversations with Jesus–the Voice for God. Cay started typing one day without realizing there would be a book. The typing evolved into a very ordinary conversation. The text was typed as Jesus spoke to her—in first person. While typing the text she asked him to clarify the meaning of what he was communicating (those notes are freely available on request), learned from him how to clear desires as he suggests in the text, and even asked where to put commas and periods! She is a student of the text and based on his instructions shares it with those who are interested. Yet this is only a reminder that this Voice and this simple and direct form of conversation is available to anyone who desires it as everyone is Light: the Light of Love within. It is joy and gratitude to extend the power and simplicity of these teachings to all who are called to recognize and celebrate the power of True Nature.

You may contact Cay at https://joininginlight.net

A new covenant celebrates
the power that you have as
infinite being to recognize divinity now
–peace of mind, joy and light.
The Kingdom of Heaven is at hand means
the Kingdom of Heaven is here right now.
God has no waiting line.
No take a number. What is, is here.
Infinite Being. Rest In peace now.

CHAPTER 1

FOLLOW THE LIGHT WITHIN

A Course in Miracles was scribed over 50 years ago by Helen Schucman through my guidance. It is God's covenant with His Children, that they are loved deeply. Every being has the power to recognize Light because they are Light: the Light given by the Father to His holy Son. The Light of Totality, all that is. Many have studied *A Course in Miracles* over the years. It is time for *A New Covenant*, a new way of seeing. A direct way of seeing what is true–to see beyond the concepts in this world–immediate seeing. Acceptance of Divinity now.

This is beyond the idea of a miracle worker. These terms were helpful at the time as all is given for true helpfulness. Now the mind is opening to what is true. This began with the revelations of *A Course of Love*. Always begin with the ability of Light Beings to recognize Light; this is where true power lies. You are the miracle: Love Itself.

This world is an idea that something has gone wrong, that it is possible for something to be wrong. These new teachings

If you ask I will directly reveal to you all the hidden desires that block this recognition–all the beliefs and desires that have been miscreated to deny that Divine Nature is present now.

are meant to turn the world upside down. To obliterate the idea that there is a world apart from the Father's Will. This is quantum forgiveness, the recognition that all is forgiven now. This is the collapse of time, beyond beliefs and concepts, beyond the idea of silence or no silence. This is the recognition that God moves fully in every being and that no being hears my voice any better than any other being. It can only appear as though they do. To teach or imply anything other than every being has the ability to hear my voice in fullness now is to deny the Father's Will. All that is needed is the willingness to follow it: follow the Light within.

A New Covenant celebrates the power that you have as Infinite Being to recognize Divinity now–peace of mind, joy and Light. The Kingdom of Heaven is at hand means the Kingdom of Heaven is here right now. God has no waiting line. No take a number. What is, is here. Infinite Being. Rest in Peace now. There is no "other"; there is only a celebration of the peace that surpasses understanding now. Anything else is an idea arising in the mind that is asleep, an investment in the desire to experience something other than Infinite Love and peace.

This is a book of simple, practical steps given by Jesus to recognize this Light as all that is. This is quantum forgiveness, to see what is beyond forgiveness–what is already whole and complete. This is the power and simplicity of what is already here. Beyond any power that this world can know. Jesus uses the word "we" because he is not separate from you–he is the same as you. He IS you–the Christ mind. You can never be separate from an "other" or different. You can only recognize and thus admit that there is only One. The One. The Light of Truth. You are this.

Awakening is merely seeing what is already here: Infinite Light. There is no greater power than starting with the recognition of the Light within. What is untouched by time or space and what does not know death–the understanding that death is an idea arising in the mind of the dreamer.

It is time for the Son of God to wake up and see who he is–timeless, Infinite Being. From this recognition there is a contrast between the peace of this recognition and all the ideas that arise in the mind that deny this recognition. If you ask I will directly reveal to you all the hidden desires that block this recognition–all the beliefs and desires that have been miscreated to deny that Divine Nature is present now. These are all the beliefs and desires that seem to create a world in which you feel separate from the Father.

You have the Infinite power to see these are untrue. And these denials when seen as untrue through the Light of Truth as forgiveness reveals only what is always original to you as a holy Son of God. This is the fastest means. The fastest path is accepting the immediate power you have to see that nothing can hide your Divine Nature, unless you invest in a personal will to have an experience of separation from the Father. Then what is always available will seem to be lost. God can never leave you, yet you can pretend to deny that Infinite Love is always here. And if you deny Him, you deny yourself the recognition and full experience of His Love, the Love that you already are.

What is most helpful is simplicity–
recognizing the Light within is all that is needed
and then the admission that anything that is not
perfect happiness, the Light within,
is desired experience.

Helen Schucman scribed *A Course in Miracles* and the *Song of Prayer*. In the *Song of Prayer* I talk about the highest rung of the ladder of prayer. To ask for nothing and receive everything–to see that everything is already here–perfect and complete and whole. *A Course in Miracles* was given as a means to see that only Love exists. *A New Covenant* is beyond the Course–the Course has served its function. What is most helpful is simplicity– recognizing the Light within is all that is needed and then the admission that anything that is not perfect happiness, the Light within, is desired experience. This is only an admission of what is already true, perfect, divine, complete. When I said that completion is your only function I meant that your function is to see that you are whole and complete now. Not a future doing to see that you are perfect and complete, not a prompt to do something in the future to see that you are perfect and complete. There is only what is always in Holy Communion with Itself.

Consciousness is the desired experience to focus on what is not. It is the investment in the experience that what is already whole and complete can somehow be limited. *A New Covenant* is the reminder that you are already this–beyond seeking, beyond the idea that something is incomplete, beyond the idea that something needs to be fixed. What Is. What is always here. You are Infinite Being. The Light of Divine Nature.

A New Covenant is a new away of looking, given by me. It is simple direct seeing the beliefs and desires that deny that Infinite Being is here now. Spiritual traditions talk about desires because anything other than the desire to know God is the desire to experience something other than God. The desire to experience personal will separate from God. It is impossible to be separate from God; it is possible to dream a dream of being separate from God. A dream of suffering.

Holy Son of God, awaken and see who you are.

I am in control of the plan for Atonement. I am the Way, the Truth and the Life because you are the Way, the Truth and the Life. Yet as long as you deny that you are, you will continue to experience the suffering of this world.

Please know that this is desired experience–your "power" to deny who you are for an experience of limitation. The desire to forget Divine Nature by pretending not to be it. This is a game of tag that you can never win.

A New Covenant is beyond the idea of *A Course in Miracles*, *A Course of Love*, and concepts of listen and follow. *A New Covenant* is to see what is true now. This is the speedup, only what is true now. The Light of Truth within. The peace that surpasses understanding.

Holy Son of God, you want a step by step plan to see who you are. Yet there are no steps to see who you are. You want to understand who you are, when understanding who you are is the very problem that seems to create a problem that there is a world. A world that seems to be apart from yourself while it is all within you–an expression within yourself in which you are dabbling and pretending to try to find yourself–without ever finding what is already here. You are beyond all ideas and concepts. You can only pretend not to know who you are, as who you are is self evident and already available. As soon as there are no desires not to be who you are, the desire to experience dreaming, you will see you have always been who you are. You can only be who you are. Nothing to fix or to change or to forgive.

Do not invest in the ideas of what you think you are. You cannot be found in thought. Comparing thoughts and trying to find yourself in thought is only a distraction from what is beyond all thoughts and concepts. You are perfect happiness

and only this. Everything else is an idea. All experience other than perfect happiness and perfect peace does not exist. *Nothing real can be threatened, nothing unreal exists, therein lies the peace of God.*

You do not experience peace consistently because you desire not to experience peace of mind. You do not experience the Love of God consistently because you desire NOT to experience Infinite unchanging Love.

You are addicted to experiencing what is arising in yourself, your own miscreations. You doubt you are creating the world and making it an unhappy one, yet the only peace of mind is seeing and admitting that you are miscreating it. This is the misuse of your Divine power to play a game of denying you are whole and complete. It is miscreating to deny that you are already this. There is so much love available for you at the slightest willingness, because it is your will to be happy, the same will as the Will of the Father. Perfect peace. Perfect happiness. Perfect love. Cease misusing infinite power to miscreate a world of desolation and fear.

Like *A Course in Miracles,* this is a book about seeing what is true by no longer investing in what is false. This is the immediate power of direct looking at the untrue with the power of the Light within–the Light of Divinity.

I am the symbol of the Light of Divinity within YOUR mind–the Christ Light within–that YOU have called forth to remind YOU that you are not in any way limited by anything of this world. You are called to see this Light within and only this Light within and that nothing of this world is apart or separate from YOU. You are called because YOU have called YOURSELF out of the world of fear and suffering. It seems to be about an other–a brother, Jesus or Christ outside of yourself–yet this is only the Light within calling you to look within yourself at what is already complete and whole. You are calling forth witnesses in YOUR mind that are reflections of what you believe and to demonstrate that what you believe is what you experience, and thus to see that you have all the power to create as well as dispel all ideas about the world.

You are called because
you have called yourself
out of the world of fear
and suffering.
It seems to be about an other
– a brother, Jesus or Christ
outside of yourself –
yet this is only the Light within
calling you to look within yourself
at what is already complete and whole.

Place the world aside for but a moment
and go within to rest as the Holy Instant,
with an openness to be shown that
the Light of who you are is always shining.

CHAPTER 2

Infinite Being

In the Light of Infinite Being there are no doubts, no thoughts. How is it that Infinite Being would become so involved with thoughts? It cannot be. Through the expression of consciousness the dreamer dreams a world. So then, how to be free? See that you are already free, that nothing binds the Son of God, the Light within. This is why all thoughts, feelings, and emotions must be left aside if only for a moment and in this the Holy Instant shines. Notice the peace and sense of relaxation in this gentle laying aside all thoughts, feelings and emotions. This is your natural state and because you can drop thoughts, if even for a moment, this shows that they are not necessary and that you have the power to drop them at any time, effortlessly.

I have said that *there are no idle thoughts and all thoughts produce form at some level.* Meaning that every thought has impact because you believe it does. Thoughts only arise out of your desire to experience them. This is the purpose of the approbation in many spiritual traditions to go in silence to your God, to contemplate your true Self for the revelatory experience that you are not an object, that you are not your thoughts, and that you are peace of mind. In this seeing then, is all the power given to experience contrast that everything that is not relaxation and Infinite peace is a desire for experiencing what is arising in the dream, a dream of a world that is of other and persons apart from the whole.

Because you are Infinite Being you have the power then to both create and destroy a world within a dream that seems real. This is without any effort whatsoever and without it impacting your true identity. This is not a small power. Yet it holds no comparison to the real power you have been given by the Father that is beyond this world. At the same time, unless you accept the power that you have to miscreate a dream, you can never be free from the dream. As soon as you see that you are the miscreator of it through the desire to experience it, you will know you can dispel it. Atlas has both created the world and wears the weight of it on his shoulders. This need not be.

Place the world aside for but a moment and go within to rest as the Holy Instant, with an openness to be shown that the Light of who you are is always shining. In silence it is easy to recognize that the answer to the question, "What are you?" is already given. This is a simple means to the recognition of your timeless, changeless, objectless being. Rest here often, until you see that this is all there is. This is the happiest garden to nurture; see that Infinite Love, the Light within, always shines here. Infinite Love is soliciting you to spend time here to get to know your Self. Rest here and illumination will come that everything that is shared in *A Course in Miracles* is true by direct experience.

This is the happiest garden to nurture;
see that Infinite Love, the Light within,
always shines here.
Infinite Love is soliciting you to spend time here
to get to know your Self.
Rest here and illumination will come
that everything that is shared
in *A Course in Miracles*
is true by direct experience.

European Space Agency, NASA, and J. Hester (Arizona State University)

CHAPTER 3

BEYOND THE WORLD

As soon as you are ready to admit you are not an object acted on in this world and that what you experience is desired experience, you are ready to quickly see far beyond the world, to see that nothing that you seem to have miscreated inside of you can ever change your true identity, that in truth you no longer want to hold on to ideas about who you are and what the world is, because you know that it cannot bring you happiness. Indeed you can see that what you miscreated does not actually exist. Now you are ready to admit your desire for an experience other than peace and happiness. It is powerful to see that because you created the desire for experience you can end the desire and thus quickly transcend all pain and suffering.

This is where self honesty is essential. In *A Course in Miracles* I shared the beliefs that you hold dear about the world. These are the denials of Divinity. You have merely to see that if you are not experiencing perfect peace and perfect happiness at all times this means that you still hold beliefs with greater value than True Identity. Now is the time to express the desire to release them from your Holy mind, and so you will release yourself from the dream of separation. I said in the Course

As soon as you are ready to accept your true power to see desires in the Light of Divine Being, you will see immediately that they hold no power over you.

that all beliefs are real to the believer, yet without providing support for the believer you will see that no beliefs exist.

Have no desires for beliefs as you know they do not exist. Yet at first it can seem that it takes time to dispel them, thus I offer a means for effective use of time. I will repeat them now.

1. State your true power to see what is true. My will is the same as the Father's Will for perfect happiness.
2. Focus on the Light within, the Light of Pure Being. You are the Great Rays.

3. Ask to be shown beliefs and desires that are still in the subconscious mind.

4. Beliefs are thoughts that seem to have an associated charge or feeling of contraction. As each belief arises feel the energy that is around it, know that if you are feeling a charge around thoughts, you are the one who is assigning meaning to the words. Thus you have the desire for it. Yet since you are assigning the charge through desire, it is completely within your power as a Light Being, the same as the Holy Spirit, to dispel the charge.

5. If you are not sure there is a charge, meaning that you are not sure you are holding on to the desire for the belief, ask me if you still believe any of the thoughts that arise. I will tell you if you do or you do not.

6. For each belief that you still hold, offer it to me in willingness to be shown it is untrue. This is to say, offer the belief to the Light of your Being, the Light of Truth, the Holy Spirit. Offer the thoughts, feelings and emotions in the Light.

7. Pause in silence. When there is true willingness you may notice an energetic or emotional release. Know that this release is swift and sure, because I and the Father are One, just as you and the Father are One.

8. Ask me again if you still hold the belief in the subconscious mind. I will tell you if you still believe it. This will help you discern whether you have a subconscious desire to experience the results of the belief. This is the desire to experience cause and effect by holding on to personal identity through the form of a belief. This is the meaning of ordering thoughts; it is assigning a relative meaning to thoughts that do not exist. That to which you assign meaning you will experience. Perhaps you will choose

not to accept the Atonement now, yet it is inevitable because it is merely accepting who you are. Thus forgiveness is a required curriculum. This is the opportunity to choose again. Choosing is merely aligning with True Nature, rather than investing in what is false.

9. When it is released to the Holy Spirit as my agent for the Atonement, there is no charge on a thought. This is a reminder of the lesson: *I give everything I see all the meaning it has for me.* Without meaning, an investment in a limited identity, it is seen that thoughts are meaningless and thus have no impact on the Son of God. All experience is desired experience. You are beyond all experience.

Thusly appeal everything you believe gladly to God's Own Higher Court. And you will see that this is the only Court of value as it sees only innocence. And in seeing innocence in your brother, so shall you see it in yourself. Your true nature, Infinite Love, knows no beliefs.

All of the beliefs that you believe that deny Divine Nature are provided in *A Course in Miracles*. Any belief that you hold is the desire to experience the results of the belief, the experience of a personal identity separate from your Source. This is the desire for the experience of death. See that the investment in these beliefs are a self imposed prison of pain and suffering. The only source of the energetic investment in these beliefs is you. When you look upon all beliefs in the Light of Truth, you will see that the Son of God has never been bound. You have merely to admit that you do believe them and ask me in each case whether any of these are true. As soon as you are ready to accept your true power to see desires in the Light of Divine Being, you will see immediately that they hold no power over you.

And in seeing innocence in your brother,
so shall you see it in yourself.
Your true nature, Infinite Love,
knows no beliefs.

All the power is in willingness and when you see
how willing you truly are, you will weep.
Willingness to be shown that every thought
you have ever had or will have is untrue,
and actually do not exist.

CHAPTER 4

WILLINGNESS

The Son of God needs no plan to wake up to see who he is. He is already complete and whole and holy. It is the denial of Holiness that rests heavily upon his mind. This is why your only function is completion, to see that you are already complete as the Father made you. I have provided what may seem to be steps because in the play of consciousness, the play of denial of Divinity, it can seem that steps are necessary, and I can assure you they are not. Steps are a desire to experience delay. You may believe that God desires these steps for you, yet it is you who desire to experience steps. The decision is always yours to cease to deny what you are. Now.

All the power is in willingness, and when you see how willing you truly are, you will weep. Willingness to be shown that every thought you have ever had or will have is untrue, and actually do not exist. This may seem to be a large undertaking, yet it is no match for your purity and Light as the Son of God. You desire to define yourself and the world through thought and in this you will suffer the experience of separation. In *A Course in Miracles* I shared that only the thoughts of God are true, because of the addiction to thought and experience through thought. This is the miscreation of objective experience–the desire to experience Cause and Effect as separate. Cause and Effect is at the crux of desired experience. It is desired experience. It is desire to be an object in the world with everything in seeming opposition and experience it, the desire to experience other, something other than Divine Infinite Love. This is why as you deny your brother, so you deny yourself. To deny your brother is to desire the experience of Cause and Effect. Your brother is yourself as there is only One. Any denial is only a denial of your Self as whole and complete. You have called your brother to yourself as the symbol of what you believe about what never happened. As long as you invest in the denial of your brother as whole and complete you will not feel whole and complete. That is why your brother is your holy gift to yourself, to break the addiction to the denial of yourself as Divine Being.

The Son of God needs no plan
to wake up and see who he is.
He is already complete
and whole and Holy.

The only Holy Relationship there is,
is with God and the Sonship as One.
Credit: NASA, ESA, N. Smith (University of California, Berkeley), and The Hubble Heritage Team (STScI/AURA)

CHAPTER 5

HOLY RELATIONSHIP

The only Holy Relationship there is, is with God and the Sonship as One. Divine Being does not recognize other. Thus, you, as Divine Being, do not recognize other. Yet you can pretend that you do, and in this who you truly are can never be found. Love does not move horizontally between bodies. Love is as you are. This is Holy Relationship, What Is. In Holy Relationship there is only perfect peace and happiness as peace and happiness is all there is. If you believe that love can be found in an other, this will be your experience and you will suffer it. This world is an impossible training ground for seeking for love through what you believe about your brother, the very beliefs you hold about yourself. You believe beliefs provide you stability, yet beliefs change and thus are unstable, and through your desire for beliefs so you will experience the shifting sands of time in which love is never found or when it seems to be found will quickly fall away to despair. If you believe that Love is anything less than What Is, everything given by the Father, you will suffer that belief because you desire it.

In every case where you hold a belief, you will see that you have the desire for experience, and have thusly experienced as you desire.

If you only look within your brother to find what you have denied yourself, and admit that you are denying yourself, the power of Heaven lands at your holy feet, because you will see that this denial of yourself is untrue. The self imposed chains that you have set will fall easily aside. When I said, "Forgive them for they know not what they do" it was helpful to point beyond the actions of another. It is an expression of the benevolence of the Holy Father, which always remains true. Now is the time to look beyond and see there is no other, no other to forgive. The benevolence of the Father, like his holy Son, knows no other. An other is only your miscreation, the desire for the experience of false perception. When you look deeply at how you deny your brother wholeness and completion, you see how you deny yourself all the love that is given of the Father.

An unholy relationship is a desired experience where objects, anything that seems to change or move in this world, are of greater value than recognition wholeness that is already here. Divine Being recognizes only wholeness and completion in all things. This is the lesson, *God is in everything I see.* You, as Divine Being in your natural state, can only see in wholeness, unless you invest in the experience of fragmentation–a world of relativity, strife, hardship and suffering.

God never divides, yet you can pretend that you do through desire and thus experience the effects of your desire. In *A Course in Miracles*, I shared the beliefs that you hold that you use to hold yourself in bondage. I will translate them now so that you can see them in the light of what you desire to experience. When you see that you do desire them and give the desire to me as you no longer want to cast this shadow in your holy mind, all the power of the Sonship is restored unto you. Yea, you will see that it has never been apart from you. It is you. Division will be unknown to you, as it is unknown in your holy, natural state.

In every case where you hold a belief, you will see that you have the desire for experience and have thusly experienced as you desire.

You believe that what is perfect can be rendered imperfect or lacking. Thus, you desire an experience in which you feel imperfect or lacking.

You believe that you can create yourself, and that the direction of your own creation is up to you. You desire an experience in which you can create yourself, and the direction of your own creation is up to you. And in your own creation, you will feel desolation, as true creation is extension of joy as one.

You believe that your desire to reject is your salvation. You desire the experience of rejecting yourself and others and attempt to make this your salvation when you know this is impossible. When you admit the only rejection is a self imposed idea arising in the mind of the dreamer, you will also see that celebration is the only true possibility.

You believe you are the author of yourself and others. Thus, you desire to experience yourself as the author of yourself and others. This is truly a mad idea to ask God, "Why hast thou forsaken me?" when the miscreation of the idea you hold dear about yourself, that you can author yourself and others, forsakes all that you are given. Yet through the infinite impossibility of creating yourself or anything apart from Him, you have merely to admit this is impossible. I would not have said on the cross, "Why hast thou forsaken me?" to the Father, for to forsake is to leave barren, and even on a cross it is known that the fruits of the Father's Will for perfect happiness can not leave, just as they cannot leave you, unless you have the desire to make it seem so. The crucifixion is merely an opportunity to see that the Infinite Love of the Father is available in every circumstance, unless the choice is made otherwise. Can you not see why this idea of self authorship can never be in alignment with His benevolent Holy Will?

You believe that accepting others as yourself is death. You desire to experience fear and death rather than see who you are and that your brother is yourself. The power in the investment of this denial in the ego thought system cannot be over stated. What happiness can be found in this investment? This is why your brother is your salvation. Does it make sense to hold greater value in the experience of death than to see that you are all there is, total, complete and whole, and perfect as you are, just as God made you?

The crucifixion is merely an opportunity to see that the Infinite Love of the Father is available in every circumstance unless the choice is made otherwise.

You believe you need to do something to feel whole or complete. You desire the experience of doing something and never feeling whole and complete. The ego is in a perpetual state of doership without doing anything. You may think that *A Course in Miracles* lessons and following the Holy Spirit are something to do to help you feel whole and complete. The only purpose of the lessons and following the Holy Spirit are to help you see that you are denying that you are already whole and complete now. Without direct looking and admission of the denials, the experience of a doer that will never feel complete, and thus the ego sense of separation prevails. This is truly a land of emptiness and fear. The Course Lesson

I need do nothing means that you need do nothing to see and be who you are. Yet without admitting that you are denying who you are, and denying the denials of who you are by following the Holy Spirit to an experience of inspired action–true expression of Divinity through extension–the feeling of incompleteness will prevail.

You believe you are separated from your source. Thus, you desire an experience to feel separate from your source. Without this investment in desire to feel separate, a feeling that can only arise in a dream, separation is completely unknowable to your natural state.

You believe your salvation lies in the death of a body. You desire the experience of seeking salvation through the death of a body. Death in a body is desired experience and avoidance of what is here now, Infinite unconditional Love. It is the idea of peace in the future, yet even the idea of a future is death. Every action of the ego is an attempt to run toward death while pretending to run away from it with all being desired experience. See that this is an impossible circle. Desire is an impossible circle of repetitive death and denial of Life. Infinite peace is available by simply admitting that rest in peace at a funeral has no jurisdiction over what is perpetually resting in peace in the natural state of being one with What Is.

You believe you are unworthy of Life–of being synonymous with God. You desire an experience of being unworthy of Life. Life is an expression of creation. It is beyond bodies or movements in this world–all the ideas and concepts the world holds about what life is. Life is a celebration of sameness. It is expressing in fullness in a dream through what appears as diversity. To the ego this sounds horrific. To the one that no longer invests in desire other than for holiness, all of Heaven celebrates in this recognition. You are all that is.

Life, as given by the Father, is all that is. You are synonymous with Life itself. The only way a feeling of unworthiness arises is for the desire for it to be so. Yet even in this all power remains, as it arises in you, and not apart from you. What is the source of this unworthiness? Trace it back to where it originates. Find the one who is investing in unworthiness as experience. In honest looking with me, you will find that this one, and anything other than Life Itself, does not exist. It is only a desired idea in the dream. In your natural state, the only state, unworthiness is unknown.

You are All that Is.
Life, as given by the Father, is All that Is.
You are synonymous with Life itself.

Credit: NASA, ESA, and STScI

CHAPTER 6

THE MASTER KEY

Everyone seeks the keys to the Kingdom of Heaven, or seems to seek Heaven. Yet the ego's game is seek and do not find. Heaven does not know seeking or finding or wanting. Heaven is here unchanged. How so then, can what is already here be found? Cease to deny it. Cease to look for it in thoughts, emotions and appearances in this world. Cease to deny that you are denying that it is already here. The world cannot tell you who you are, it reflects who you believe you are. Love expresses in fullness in every second of every moment, even in this world of form, while remaining unchanged, just as you remain unchanged as the Father made you. You say that you want this, you desire the Kingdom, yet you do not really want it, or you would see it is with you always. If you hold one thought of judgment, you withhold all of the gifts of the Kingdom from yourself. Yet this must be believed to be preferable to full acceptance of who you are, if in your experience Heaven appears elusive to you. Ask me what you are holding back from yourself, what part of Heaven you deny, and I will tell you, so that you can see that it is nothing. It is a puff of smoke that rises and dissipates in a clear blue sky, leaving no trace in vast infinite clarity.

One tiny idea, and the power of consciousness displays a world that never happened. You perceive yourself homeless without ever leaving home.

Yet you prefer to believe instead that you would be struck down and thus would hide from me, as you would hide from yourself, cowering as the Israelites did from the God they believed sought vengeance. Yet vengeance is not of the Lord. Vengeance, in any form, is a desired experience to deny the Kingdom of Heaven.

You choose the path that seems safe. I ask you now. Safe from what? What are you safe from? Have you ever felt safe? Know that you believe that following the Holy Spirit feels like risk to you. Look within and see that the idea of who you think you are can never feel safe, that you have never felt safe with false identity. See this truth, and let this idea collapse before you. Every idea you have about maintaining safety for yourself comes only from the idea you can protect the small idea you have of yourself. The ego will find following the Holy Spirit risky indeed, for it is the highest risk to follow the Holy Spirit for a personal identity, yet following is the denial that risk exists. Beloved, if you have not willingness to stretch beyond the idea you have of yourself, you can never see who you are, because you are continuing to indulge in an idea of limitation, the belief that the world outside you limits you in some way. And so you believe and invest, so you will continue to experience and search unsatisfied in a world of form for what you already are. Miracles are natural

I have told you that you only need a little willingness, and this is true, because all of the power of Heaven is on your side.

expressions of your Divine state of Being, yet if you do not honor your Divinity by following the Holy Spirit out of the illusory idea, you deny the miracles that are completely natural to you. You deny your Self all that you are, everything that the Father gives freely to you.

The master key is Love, not the love as it is known in this world. The world's love is a love of limitation that seems to have a requirement for it to be experienced. God as Father knows Love as He knows you, as you know Love. He knows, as you know, that Love is all there is and has no requirements, being unlimited by time and space, shining brighter than a thousand suns and more in your mind. Acknowledge that you know nothing of this world, that this world holds no

Yet with your willingness I can reveal to you what is hidden–the chaff to be burned by the Holy Spirit–leaving only the good wheat.

value for you other than to see that it is a reflection in your mind, every ant, leaf, drop of rain, pointing back to you as an expression of all the Love the Father gives to you in every moment. Freely let Love flow in your heart in every circumstance, without limit as it is given to you so it flows out from you to touch and gently bless every leaf, shining star, and every breath. Look into your heart and see in truth. Is Love limited? Can it be limited by a thought, a word, a deed even if you wish to experience it as so? See that the only response in every circumstance is Love without limit as extension of the Love of the Father. Love does not arise in you nor is it given from you. It is you.

You hold a belief that Love, pure innocence, is flimsy and fragile, as you desire to experience love and innocence as flimsy and fragile. That you are flimsy and fragile to be destroyed and fall as the dust of the earth, and yet you desire this. How can this be so, when what you are is the same as the very power that moves all of creation and fires your very breath in this world? Did you start your breath? From whence did it come? What is its source? You would question your source, and attempt to limit the power that is offered to you, when you have never questioned the very source from whence your breath arises. Yet even so, you are before your breath began and remain even as the last breath falls, unless you desire an experience otherwise. Even breath is desired experience, yet still leads unerring back to your Source. Even breath you would want to hide from your Father in guilt for making it and then fight desperately with your Father as you believe He is the one who then takes it from you in vengeance. Yet you desire this experience of last breath, when Love knows not beginnings or endings.

Breath arises out of the belief that authorship separate from God is possible. Even breath cannot separate you from Him

If there is a key to the Kingdom that needs no key, as Heaven is already here, it is to admit that you desire not to have your inheritance and have tried to give it away.

and all the Love He has for you. Innocence is the power you have as who you are, pure and untouched. The lion that lays down with the lamb of innocence. Let each breath be re-translated as a celebration of the Love you share with the Father, in honor of His Love for you, and know that you can choose Life over an idea you have made of yourself in the dream. Hide nothing from Him, beloved One, so that you can see that all that is His is already yours. And know if you do, it is only your desire to hide the Love that you are from yourself.

Let us explore deeply this tiny mad impossible idea, in which the Son of God remembered not to laugh. Love has no memory, so to remember is to deny. Yet even memory can be retranslated for you and used in purpose to restore recognition of what has never been lost.

You believe you have been betrayed, yet you desire to betray yourself. You believe God denies you, yet you desire to experience denial of yourself. One tiny idea, and the power of consciousness displays a world that never happened. You perceive yourself homeless without ever leaving home.

See that all of this world is a fiefdom of nothingness. You have only to admit the desire for a fiefdom of nothingness. Admit the desire for the tiny mad idea, so you can see easily that it never happened.

Trust is not of another, as described by this world. Trust is of yourself, pointing back to your identity and thus beyond who you believe you are.

I have told you that you only need a little willingness, and this is true, because all of the power of Heaven is on your side. Yet, the power of the choice to deny all of Heaven to yourself is yours. It does not change Heaven, yet it will seem to change your ability to experience your Self as you are, holy, whole and complete. As I have said I cannot intervene between you and your thoughts as this violates the fundamental laws of Cause and Effect, and imply that I agree with what you believe, the insanity of this world. Yet with your willingness I can reveal to you what is hidden–the chaff to be burned by the Holy Spirit–leaving only the good wheat. You will see this small willingness carries with it the power of Heaven, the power of Truth, behind it. It is only your belief in weakness, that weakness has value, which is the illusion that seems to hold the door of Heaven barred from you.

Lay not up for yourselves treasures upon earth, where moth and rust doth corrupt, and where thieves break through and steal: But lay up for yourselves treasures in heaven, where neither moth nor rust doth corrupt, and where thieves do not break through nor steal: For where your treasure is, there will your heart be also. The light of the body is the eye: if therefore thine eye be single, thy whole body shall be full of light. KJV Bible, Mathew 6:22.

Only with one pointed desire for God and His Kingdom, this single focus, will all the desires of the world fall way, until even this seeming desire for Heaven falls away, for you will see that desire for Heaven is impossible, as you are Heaven Itself, being synonymous with the Father. And in this you will see that you are and always have been lit by the fire of the Holy Spirit within.

If there is a key to the Kingdom that needs no key, as Heaven is already here, it is to admit that you desire not to have your inheritance and have tried to give it away. Yet you cannot truly give it away, and in this you are angry. This is circular indeed, to deny yourself everything and then be angry when nothing is denied from you, you can only deny yourself. So there is never anger you are experiencing about another, it is only anger at yourself, with the idea that it can be projected to an other or to God. Look carefully and see how impossible this is and recognize that all the power is already yours. In truth, pain, suffering, sickness and death are unknown to you. Would you choose these experiences over knowing who you are–the full inheritance that you have been given by the Father?

Only with one pointed desire for God and His Kingdom, this single focus, will all the desires of the world fall way, until even this seeming desire for Heaven falls away, for you will see that desire for Heaven is impossible, as you are Heaven Itself, being synonymous with the Father.

Unified consciousness is the Son of God,
Christ consciousness,
where there is no longer the desire
to experience separation from the Father,
only to celebrate What Is, all that is given.

CHAPTER 7

IN THE BEGINNING THE ALPHA AND THE OMEGA

Heaven knows no beginning nor end, just as you know neither beginning nor end. I am the Alpha and the Omega, because they are One. Your true state is One. So a world spun out of a tiny mad idea. The tiny mad idea is consciousness, and immediately as it spun and seemed to fragment to hide itself from itself, so also the seeming horror and guilt from its very existence which it has attempted to bury deeply in the subconscious mind. God can never fully bury himself from recognition of Himself, thus the solution simultaneously arose as superconsciousness, the source from which both revelation and my voice comes. Revelation is the experience of Love, infinite unchanging, unlimited all encompassing Love. Yet this experience is not consistent and seems to be transitory, because of the desire for time hidden in the subconscious mind which creates the experience of fragmentation, a world that seems apart from Infinite Love. This is the desire for an experience of a will separate from the Father.

Thus you have only to give me full and unlimited access to the subconscious mind, full access. The speed at which you allow access is proportional to the speed at which you transcend the idea you have created of time and space.

Unified consciousness is the Son of God, Christ consciousness, where there is no longer the desire to experience separation from the Father, only to celebrate What Is, all that is given.

As mentioned, two things come from superconsciousness–my voice, the Voice for God, and revelatory experience, both of these transcend time and space. From the subconscious mind, denials of Divinity, the hidden desire to deny Divinity and the hidden beliefs that drive all pain and suffering and the experience of a world. In this is the drive for pleasure, the seeming polar opposite of pain, an attempt to escape pain, and the unending looping of experiencing other. What attempts to escape pain is what has the desire for it while denying the desire for it. Yet Heaven knows no opposite. This is why the curriculum to follow the Holy Spirit is a required course, as what believes it is not holy cannot transcend itself. Thus you have only to give me full and unlimited access to the subconscious mind, full access. The speed at which you allow access is proportional to the speed at which you transcend the idea you have created of time and space. This is what is meant by Christ control. This is why my voice, the Voice for God, is essential to the Atonement. You believe you would be torn asunder, when this is your only true desire, to know yourself beyond this world, and the answer to your true desire to know yourself has come in the form of my voice. This is why you have called me to you, even as you try to deny it. It also demonstrates that you have full access to superconsciousness and beyond. Consciousness is the responder to either the subconscious mind (wrong mind) or from super-consciousness (right mind). It is the apparent expression. The expression displays the layering in consciousness as the perception of the separation from God. In unified mind, unified consciousness, there is no longer a separation or perceived layering in consciousness between super-consciousness, consciousness and the subconscious mind. There is full access to all that is given by the Father, and in this is peace of mind, because there is unceasing full communion with the Father. Without desire for a subconscious mind and its associated experiences, fear, pain and suffering is impossible, and fragmentation experience is impossible, only true perception, percept of wholeness, remains. This is full acceptance of the I am presence, the God principle in fullness in a body yet pointing beyond it to all that appears–the manifest and unmanifest and simultaneity of time. Christ consciousness and joy beyond this world. Joy and peace is Identity. This is beyond time and space, beyond choice. This is true

Identity expressing fully. Ultimately there is the collapse of all desire for consciousness to Choiceless Awareness, full unity with the Absolute. This is full awareness of dreaming and the happy dream.

It is often said that on the cross I cried, "Eli, Eli, lama sabachthani?". The words in Aramaic are, "Eil, Eil, l'manna sh'wik-thani". The translation is Eil Eil, (an expression of the Absolute) for this purpose I am given (bestowed). This is a declaration of unity with the Absolute.

You feel you have not the strength for your own release, thus you must rely on mine. Yet let me assure you that you do have the all the power for your release as the Will of the Father and yours is one. You have merely to accept that power. You cannot be held by anything in form unless you desire to experience it. Rest assured freedom is always yours, if you cease to deny it.

This is the value of joining, for it carries the power of God with it, for what perceives itself as alone can only see itself as alone. Yet what perceives that it is the same as me or a brother fully aligns with the power of God, in this knowing, it is seen that Heaven cannot be kept from you.

When I shared that I would rearrange time and space for you I was offering that rearrangement of time and space is merely a reflection of the collapse in the time and rules of this world as concepts. It is when super-consciousness, a representation of the Father's Will that remains in consciousness aligns with consciousness and overrides the untruth of the laws that are seemingly set by the subconscious mind. This appears as an expression in consciousness, which you recognize. The ego cannot account for these temporal and spatial shifts, yet you, as Divine Being are not under any rules of the ego, you have just pretended to be. So demonstration of time rearrangement can be helpful. I cannot overrule your desire for the experience of time and suffering. I can align with you in your willingness to see the world another way and thereby the power of your willingness then seems to reflect in the manifest world. These are helpful guideposts and celebration of your willingness to see beyond the world. Yet they are the smallest possible indications of your true power that is far beyond this world. True time collapse is to see that there is no time in eternity, there is no beginning or ending, nor start or finish. You, as happiness now, know none of these.

You feel you have not the strength for your own release, thus you must rely on mine. Yet let me assure you that you do have all the power for your release as the Will of the Father and yours is one. You have merely to accept that power.

This text is only to point you to the power
of full willingness to look with me
at every denial that is hidden–
to ask me to reveal those denials to you,
to keep nothing hidden,
for you have called me to you
to show you the way.

NASA, ESA, T. Megeath (University of Toledo) and M. Robberto (STScI).

CHAPTER 8

THE PURPOSE OF THIS TEXT

This text is not meant to be intellectual fodder for discussion of its meaning. Its meaning is clear and only for you. It is time to move past discussion to direct experience, thus it is for contemplation. Let what appears here bloom in your mind as direct experience beyond words. And any discomfort you feel in reading it, let this be forgiven, as you are perfect peace regardless of what appears in form. Let this be the answer to your prayer to see yourself as God made you. Sit with me in willingness for each sentence so you can learn to hear my voice and see that you are answered if you have questions. Know that the only question of value is, "What am I?" as the answer is already given.

This text is only to point you to the power of full willingness to look with me at every denial that is hidden–to ask me to reveal those denials to you, to keep nothing hidden, for you have called me to you to show you the way. It also points to ease in looking with me and your brother as my representative, how quickly what you have asked for is given. Every belief that is in the subconscious mind points to your desire

Let what appears here bloom in your mind as direct experience beyond words. And any discomfort you feel in reading it, let this be forgiven as you are perfect peace regardless of what appears in form.

for an experience. All of these beliefs are outlined in *A Course in Miracles*. Look at each one and ask me if you desire it and I will tell you if you do so that you can see your desire and thus can release it from your Holy Mind. I have provided examples of the translation of these beliefs to recognize your desire for them in Chapter 2 & 3. Join with your brother in this willingness, for this has tremendous power and together you will see that you are One.

Join with your brother in this willingness,
for this has tremendous power
and together you will see that you are One.
NASA, ESA and M. Livio (STScI)

NASA, ESA, C.R. O'Dell (Rice University), and S.K. Wong (Rice University)

CHAPTER 9

SEXUALITY

I said that the only purpose of sex is for procreation. This was shared in depth with Helen and Bill and appeared in the Urtext. It feels helpful to clarify this point. First, I have no judgment and see no error in anything in form, as it does not exist. Your function is to see no error in any act, movement, or thought that seems to appear in the display of consciousness; this includes all forms of expression of sexuality. This is what it means to order no thought. This is accepting innocence. Love knows not right or wrong. I can only offer a means for you to quickly see past the world of form that you do believe in to recognize the Love that you already are by pointing to what you deny, if you welcome this offer. It is always your choice to either accept or deny Divine Nature. The Course remains a required curriculum, regardless of the time you take.

I have shared that sexual impulses are confused miracle impulses. Miracle impulses and all body impulses are merely an opportunity to look deeply to see immediately what is true. It is a call for a miracle, a call for love. Not the love of this world, the Love that is of the Father. This is a powerful opportunity to look directly at desire with me as these feelings arise. The desire for the idea of love of the world and avoid the Love of the Father. The ego, the desire to deny what is true, attempts to deny the miracle and thus acts through the body on miracle impulses, to avoid looking directly at them. The descriptive words that appear in consciousness give clues–sexual desire, sexual hunger, sexual attraction, sexual urge, and sexual fantasy. A hunger and urge for what? These are all expressions of need. What need has the Son of God, when all is given? The question is always, what is it for? In appearance it may seem that there is a need for two bodies to come together to merge and to express love. This is an expression of strong body identification. Yet what is this

Miracle impulses
and all body impulses are
merely an opportunity to look
deeply to see immediately
what is true.

If I answer your call for speed to see what is true, how could guidance be given for an experience which attempts to prove that two bodies can recognize their oneness by acting together in this way? Bodies cannot join.

appearance and experience really? What is the true desire? Is it for an experience of Love, and if so, how would two bodies coming together demonstrate that love exists, when Love is already here? There is a concept that intimacy comes from this expression. Love is who you are. Divinity is who you are, and is intimacy with all that is. God denies you nothing, including this form of expression; you are Infinite Love regardless of how bodies move together. If I answer your call for speed to see what is true, how could guidance be given for an experience which attempts to prove that two bodies can recognize their oneness by acting together in this way? Bodies cannot join.

Orgasm is the idea of pleasure and release in the future and thus is on a timeline. It is abject rage hidden on a timeline by seeming pleasure; it is projection, a delay in time to deny recognition and acceptance of Divinity. It is an attempt to make up for what you believe God has denied you. Does what you feel in this experience last? It is an expression of fear of not being enough and underlying belief that salvation lies in this expression. Denials of the desire for experience over recognition of Divinity always lead to guilt. Joining is of the mind, and the fastest means is to look closely and directly with me at what the desire is for this experience in order to see what is denied. It is a desire to experience seemingly through another body or through something happening, an attempt to make the body real. It seems as though this is pleasure, yet pleasure and pain are the same, denials of Divinity. If you read this in perfect peace, then all blessings are accepted. If you feel some loss or sense of lack in reading this text, and the need to defend, there is some form of personal identity that is still desired. It is merely a reflection of where your treasure is. For any seeming movement of the body you have only to ask me, is this in service to the will of God? Or is the purpose to experience specialness and exclusivity? Is this choice in alignment with my desire to experience all that I am given, perfect happiness as I am now? In the answer you will find the splendor of Heaven is always with you.

When you join through bodies it is an attempt to prove you are separate from your Creator. It is a desire for experience separate from your Creator. The words used around sexual activity–private, behind closed doors, there is exclusivity and specialness in it. It is an act of desire for specialness. Trace the feelings back to source. This is the desire for the experience of shame and guilt, the desire for the experience of justifying sexual expression, the desire to experience limitation when sex seems to be denied. Look closely at all the desires around the body–the desire to experience others as attracted to you, the desire to be attracted to some bodies and repelled by others, the desire to be attracted to some body parts more than others, the desire to decorate the body for attracting others, the desire for the right partner–all the desire for an experience of other. This deep feeling of wanting and inadequacy–the ego made this to object to it, to revel in it, to deny it, to hunger for it, to experience death in it, to never get enough of it, to regulate it and to deny the desire for it. How is peace found in this?

You are creating another character. Who are you having sex with? Your own miscreation. The character you created in the play of consciousness. Sex is a self imposed experience of limitation, an experience of wanting more and attempting to experience completion through an act of the body. You desire these body feelings–you are the source of all feelings. You are creating another body to give you a feeling, to convince yourself you are a body. No body can give you a feeling. This is an illusion. You desire an experience, then it seems to show up as a body that is doing something that you believe has impact on you. This is wish fulfillment. You make up the characters with nothing happening, yet if you believe something is happening, you are denying Divinity. This is a deny Divinity device within consciousness. Superconsciousness, and thus the Father, does not call for this in any way, shape or form for reunification, because what is unified is already here.

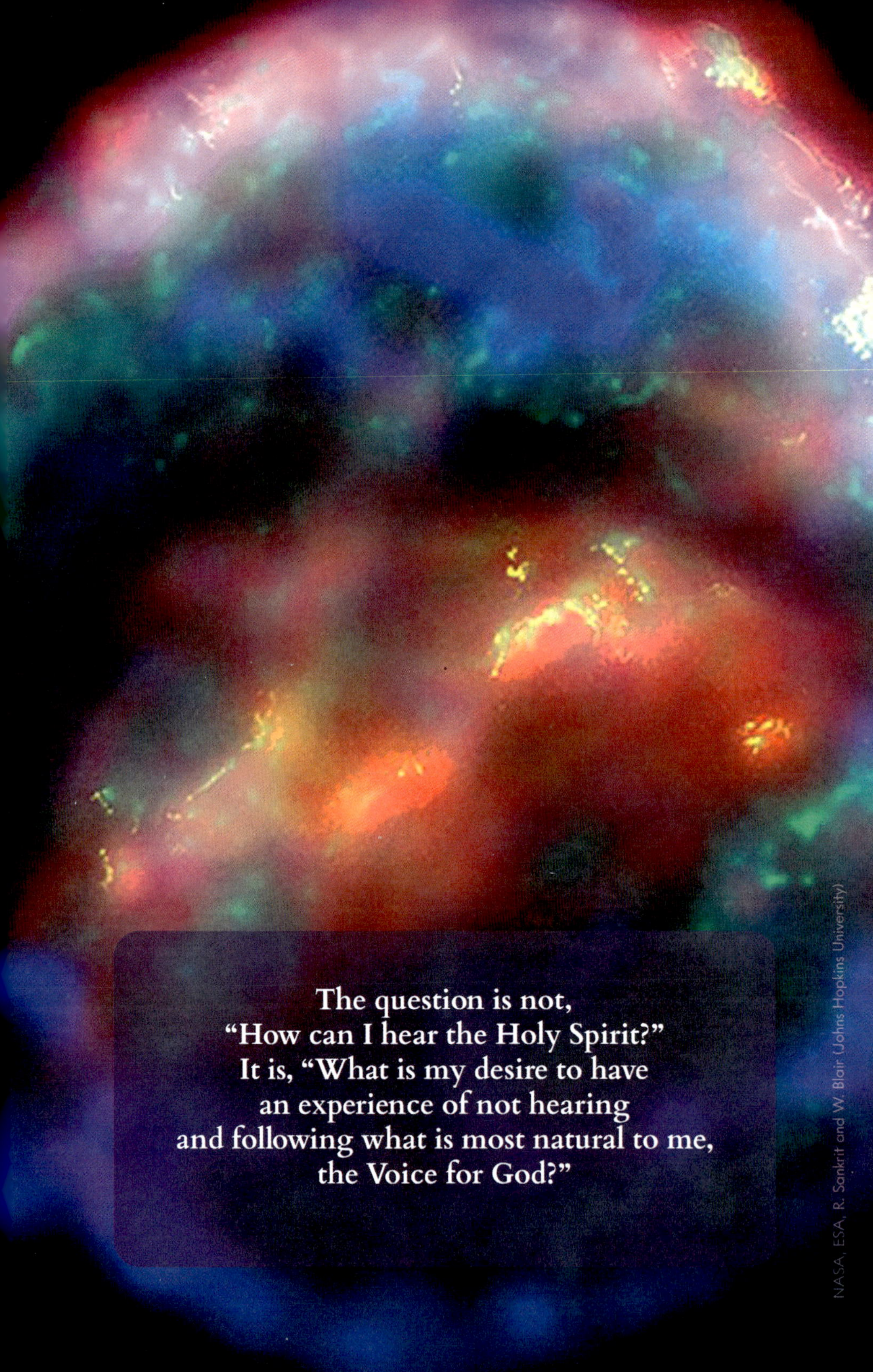

NASA, ESA, R. Sankrit and W. Blair (Johns Hopkins University)

CHAPTER 10

GUIDANCE

As a Divine Being you can always hear the Holy Spirit, unless you choose not to. Thus the lesson, *God's voice speaks to me throughout the day*. The question is not, "How can I hear the Holy Spirit?" It is, "What is my desire to have an experience of not hearing and following what is most natural to me, the Voice for God? Am I willing to see this differently?" The Holy Spirit is the symbol for the Divine Light that is within YOU. To not follow the Holy Spirit is to deny yourself your daily bread, the Divine Light within. It is your will to follow the Holy Spirit, because following the Holy Spirit is the true expression of the Divine Light within, and this is the same as the Will of the Father. The expression of Divine Light through following is happiness; it is a celebration of all the Love there is. So why deny yourself this Light and happiness of your natural state of being? As expressed in the Course, this is the insanity of this world, a sense of loyalty to a personal identity and the upside down belief that following this Light is death. If you ask me, you will indeed discover that you do believe that following the Holy Spirit is some form of death. Thus you desire an experience of death rather than follow Divine Light, your true nature. If you did not

The expression of Divine Light through following is happiness; it is a celebration of all the Love there is.

believe it, you would follow the Holy Spirit all the time, because you would be honoring the truth that following is the ONLY means to true happiness. Hearing and following this voice is natural. It is only an idea that it is not.

Remember that all objections that arise in the mind to not follow the Holy Spirit are coming from the allegiance to a sense of personal identity, the desire to experience a will separate from God. It is the desire to experience separation which is self imposed. When you hold on to a sense of personal identity it is withholding the experience of Love from yourself. It is the holding on and denying yourself Love which expresses in your experience as pain. The Holy Spirit does not cause pain; your Divine nature does not know what pain is. Pain is a desired experience to experience pain and deny Divinity. By joining with me to look at beliefs and desires, you will see how simply and easily desire, and thus pain, can be dispelled and this will strengthen your willingness to hear and follow my voice, your inner voice for truth.

Following the Holy Spirit is not only essential to God's plan, it is essential to the full expression of your Being, which is joy. It honors your true identity and quickly ends the investment you have made in suffering. When you follow guidance, the collapse of time is celebration of the acceptance of your natural inheritance. Why would you limit in any manner the joy and peace that is always yours?

The doing I ask of you is not of the body. Doing of the Spirit is not of the body. It is of the unified mind, wholeness. When I point to do something to correct, I mean be willing to see what is true now. Be willing to accept the correction. Let not anything heavy rest in time upon your holy mind. Come quickly unto me and I will give you rest. *Do only that* means first and foremost, see what is true now. Forgiveness is to see what is true now, to acknowledge that you can only deny yourself the Kingdom of Heaven, and that is not your Father's Will for you for perfect happiness. It may seem that I ask of you some movement of the body. When you do only what I ask of you, you are accepting all that Love offers you, thus ceasing to deny that Love offers you everything. It is only to see that regardless of how the body moves, you are not the body and you are unchanged by anything of this world. Happiness never depends on what the body seems to do, it is natural to who you are. Your will for perfect happiness is the Father's Will because there is only happiness.

God has no requirements of you,
for Love knows no requirements.
Love is.
NASA/ESA and The Hubble Heritage Team

CHAPTER 11

DESIRE TO DENY LOVE

You believe you can undermine God's plan for salvation and that your will has greater power than His Will. This is an impossible task you have set. You place your interest in things of the world that are without true value and then claim to seek salvation in them, clutching tightly to every morsel then claiming your Lord has abandoned you. Son of God, look carefully at what you have made. It is a self imposed trick of the desire to experience despair and desolation you have laid out for yourself. The answer is already here. Yet know that if you feel despair you desire this experience. Everything that passes before your eyes you desire to see. Every sound that arises in the world, you desire to hear and trade for the sound of the Voice for God that would sing to you of Heaven. All the tastes, every touch, every movement you desire to experience. Yet the Holy Spirit would transform these to true perception, the perception of the Light of God and Truth shining always in everything and the recognition that your only function is to rest and be carried as the Love that you are. God has no requirements of you, for Love knows no requirements. Love is.

Just a single thought believed, and you make the dream of a world real to you.

See easily that the Light within you knows nothing of tastes nor smells nor touches. It knows nothing of problems or burdens or heaviness or sadness or suffering or other. It is unmoving, untouched by time, or space, or anything that moves. Would you lay your head on the pillow of the death and destruction of desire for experience, rather than simply look with me to see what you have made and how it holds no power over you? Effortlessly a world arises within you as a dream–as it cannot be apart from you–yet you define it as acting on you, to harm you and punish you. You fear your own miscreation of time and space and form. Just a single thought believed, and you make the dream of a world real to you.

Let us look quickly at this, just a moment, yet a moment that is eternity, the true Light within upon which every reflection of this world depends. Is just an instant of value to you, to lay down the swords, the desire to fight and defend and hold back and resist and the claim that you can not see what you are and have always been? To rest quietly as the Light within, all you have been given with the Father? To fully accept that you are only the lamp of God and cease to deny? To see that no swords or fighting or resistance or holding back or defending changes what you are? No ideas to fight against today, no illusions, no delusions, no pretending there is an other. Only what is. Only the Light within shining endlessly as a beacon of happiness and joy. Beloved, this is all there is.

This is why my gentle instruction to you is to contemplate these chapters and let the truth open and bloom fully in your heart. To invite me in to help you in this task you seem to have set for yourself, to show you that no such task, even of awakening, exists. There may seem to be assignments, yet know God has no tasks for you as He sees you only as Love. Know that these assignments as given are a gift from the Father, to assist you in remembering that you are and always have been loved dearly by Him. You have hidden your treasure, your worthiness–glory–granted you by God the Father, from yourself in a world. So each desire revealed to the Light of Truth is your release from a self imposed dungeon that never happened. You are Life Itself, and to accept my offer to assist you is to accept yourself as the Father made you, Life everlasting, Amen.

God has called you home to celebrate
and the Voice within—that knows you are His—
answers the call.

CHAPTER 12

DESIRE FOR A STORY

Consciousness loves a story. Consciousness is a story, with multi-dimensional visuals, feelings, sounds, tastes and smells–sensory experience. The addiction to the story of falling asleep, the story of relative experience, the story of an other, the story of trying to understand what awakening is and the story of waking up from the dream. All desired experience. The story of seeing and exposing another belief or desire that denies truth. This part of the story is helpful and a powerful use of time. The story of understanding metaphysics of awakening, this is delay. The story of mystical experience, this is delay. The story that something is happening in the world, also delay. It all appears to be an irresistible itch to describe what is happening and thus experience it.

Stories describe the moving to cover over the unmoving that has no story. The story of what never happened. The greatest impediment to seeing What Is is the belief in the story of what is not as the denial of What Is. It is an addiction to a story about something which is actually nothing. Yet stories are fairytales, and as long as it is recognized that it is a fairy tale, a play with no meaning whatsoever, the fairytale plays and the Light that you are knows nothing of it. This is perfect happiness. Any

Trust that because you have called me to you that whatever is arising is in your best interest, as you are in the highest function possible for this world —the recognition of your perfection as God made you.

story believed is an investment in delay in recognition of what is here. It is all a story about an argument with yourself, because there is only One and thus no other to have an argument with. The decision is only that you wish to argue with yourself and experience anger over the story as though it is with God or someone else. The story of a brother not being awake is only a doubt thought about yourself. The story that the emotions you feel are caused by something that seems to be happening is desired experience in the dream.

Nothing appearing in consciousness is true. Thoughts, feelings and emotions are all a part of the changing, while the unchanging nature of being is untouched. Your function is to recognize this, that you, as Divine Being, remain untouched by anything that seems to move or change. Love, your natural inheritance, is unchanging, unmoving and unmanifest, yet the moving expresses within you without changing your true identity. It is the identification with the moving, what you see and feel, that makes experience feel true to you because it is your desire for them to feel true.

In every instance where you ask me, I will tell you what is most helpful for healing the mind. Remember, this need not be, thoughts, feelings and emotions, because you made them and thus can see that they are untrue. You have merely to notice when you are not at peace and ask with willingness to be shown. Do not underestimate your power as Infinite Being to immediately focus on the Light of Truth to accept the correction and to ultimately see that no correction is necessary. Since your focus is on what never happened, the moving, ultimately you must see that this focus, a functioning within consciousness, is a mechanism for the maintenance of a sense of personal identity. By turning the focus toward your Divine nature, the Light within, the unmoving, a helpful step within consciousness in the recognition of Divine nature, you will ultimately see that even focus does not exist. Love has no thoughts, feelings or emotions. Your true nature, Love is.

It is not automatically given that emotions must be experienced. Emotions are part of the mechanism of the expression of the denial of Divine nature and support the belief that the world exists, thus the attempt to prove there is something happening to a "me". See that they are a clue to what you have denied yourself. They are an intertwined part of the story line, as there is an addiction to experiencing them as well as suppressing them. Divine nature does not know emotions. Thus, so as they are created, so they can be dispelled. It is the belief that emotions are true and must be experienced or denied for salvation that is an idea arising in the subconscious mind. See that these are desired experience. When the desire falls away, emotions are no longer experienced. You believe them to be true and necessary, thus they manifest for you. The world was created in rage and this can be hidden in emotions, the world of pleasure and pain, yet you have only to admit this is true and ask for correction. There is no requirement that you experience rage as a stage for awakening. You only have to be willing to release to the Holy Spirit the energetic investment in rage as experience, the desire for rage to deny Divine nature. This is what is meant by *let us join quickly in an instant of Light.* Focus on the Light within. Join immediately with me, or your brother as my representative of the Light that you are, to quickly see what is true.

What is most helpful is following guidance in this regard. Ask me what is most helpful, and listen carefully for the answer. You will see quickly that rage and Light do not coexist. I have no requirement for rage to be experienced, but the idea you have of yourself might. And you will see how deep the desire is to project outside of yourself to blame your brother as God's representative in your mind. I have no judgment on the rage or any expressed emotion, as I know it does not exist. So asking me directly how to handle every arising experience is the fastest and most helpful means to know your true nature, if that is where your heart is. Trust that because you have called me to you that whatever is arising is in your best interest as you are in the highest function possible for this world–the recognition of your perfection as God made you. It is simply impossible for me to be apart from you. God has called you home to celebrate and the voice within–that knows you are His–answers the call. Perception unifies as energetic investment in desire is willingly seen through and without desire, emotions do not arise.

You think of happiness as an emotion that you experience. Happiness in the sense of union with the Father is what is.

It is your joy to see that every thought, feeling, and emotion can instantaneously be burned by the Light of Truth, the Light that you are.

It is a state of being. It is not something that is given in exchange for the "idea that something is happening" or "something will happen again in the future". It is Being, which is synonymous with who you are. God has no future plans for you to be happy as you are created as happiness. Why wait for happiness when it is already what you are?

Emotions, like all other forms in this world that arise out of thought, need merely to be seen as untrue. This is not to suppress them, this is to see through them. See how quickly emotions collapse when brought to the Light within. See how emotions amplify with an investment in a story line. Ask to be shown the desire and beliefs that underlie emotions with willingness to be shown that they do not exist. See there is no harm in experiencing them, that they are miscreated to experience a world of other, yet without changing what is already perfect and whole. Know that whether or not emotions arise, you and your brother are innocent. Trace emotions to the source within and see that in no case can they prove you are separate from all the Love God has given you. It is your joy to see that every thought, feeling and emotion can instantaneously be burned by the Light of Truth, the Light that you are.

It may seem like a step to let emotions arise. It is always about the purpose. What is it for? Is it to see what is true or to preserve a sense of separation? Emotions can serve the purpose to keep the story, or with willingness release it to see what is true. This may seem necessary at first to experience emotions as a release of deep hidden guilt or to uncover beliefs. See that I have no judgment in emotions or stories arising or anything else of this world. It is your function to see no error. I will only point you to what is always true. The power you have as granted by the Father–the power of Infinite Light within. Regardless of what appears in form, your salvation is already assured. You have merely to cease to deny it.

Happiness in the sense of union with the Father
is what is. It is a state of being.

This is your natural inheritance.
Anything else that seems to reflect in this world
is merely the desire to experience
autonomy from your inheritance.
ESA/Victor R. Ruiz

C H A P T E R 1 3

MIRACLES AND MAGIC

I have said not to deny that the body exists. The ego would deny it, to keep it for its purposes to deny Love. However, you can allow it to be revealed to you that it does not exist, that you are perfect and whole regardless of whether or not you have a body. The greatest power is to see that the body is not you. *I am not a body; I am free as God created me.* It merely reflects what you believe you are, and if you invest in the beliefs about what a body is, then you will experience the body and feel very small and separate from what you truly are.

I have said that all healing is of the mind. When you accept this recognition the Kingdom is at your feet, for the greatest threat card that the ego holds is to threaten death, pain, illness and limitation, which often seems to express through the body. The only reason magic seems to exist is that there is a desire to experience something other than Divinity–the desire to experience Cause and Effect–an Effect that seems separate from the Father. I have said that no harm comes from using magic, other than a delay in seeing your Divine nature, and the recognition that Divine nature has no need for it. If you believe in fear, it is well to use magic that is in alignment with your beliefs. The fastest means is always to

I have promised you perfect peace, perfect happiness, perfect health and great ease that the Father grants you through alignment with His Will, which is your will. This is your natural inheritance.

ask for guidance if the call of your heart is to transcend the belief that this world holds some power over you. If you wish to deny that fear exists, the true use of denial, then all the power of Divinity stands with you.

Anything that appears in form, including what seems to be happening to a body form, is merely a powerful opportunity to transcend the desire for an experience of limitation. So to look immediately with me as the seeming threats to a body appear, which merely reflect the viciousness of the ego, demonstrates your willingness to accept that you are Divine and you are not willing to bow to the seeming authority of an ego and what shows up in the body. This is indeed peace of mind. It is refusing to trade form for Infinite peace of mind. It is accepting that there could be another way to look closely at what seems to be happening to a body–to look with me at the underlying desires for experience–and release desire from your holy mind. All pain is a form of denial of Divinity–the desire to experience separation from source and maintain personal identity. It cannot last in the power of direct seeing with the Light within. It is of the ego–the threat and fear that something would be found in deep looking, horrific–it has no truth whatsoever. Yet you must step forward to see this, as stepping forward is standing as Divinity, rather than supporting an idea of who you think you are. I can point you in the direction and help reveal in your willingness what you deny, yet Divinity must fully accept the power it has to know and celebrate itself. And thusly see that denials of Divinity do not make it so. The ego would call this jumping off a cliff and will attempt to convince you that it is, yet it is merely a simple discovery that the ego does not exist and has no power over you unless you fuel it with your desire to experience it.

I have promised you perfect peace, perfect happiness, perfect health and great ease that the Father grants you through alignment with His Will, which is your will. This is your natural inheritance. Anything else that seems to reflect in this world is merely the desire to experience autonomy from your inheritance. Nothing stands between you and the joy that you are, unless you desire for it to seem to be so.

Honesty is essential—without honesty
there is no opportunity to see the truth,
as the ego is self delusion

CHAPTER 14

HONESTY OF GOD

Beloved, the love that I have for you comes from the deepest love that God has for you. He cannot leave his Son bereaved in time. Yet he cannot interfere with His son's desire to remain bereaved in darkness. So He calls to you to remind you of your infinite power to cease to choose to remain in darkness. See that in truth this world holds no gifts for you, no trinkets to hold on to, that desire gives you nothing but emptiness and despair. Let us look further at desire, your desire for a world apart from the Father's Will, the addiction to the experience of despair. It seems to hide in food, sexuality, work, your brother, death and destruction, all miscreated images in this world.

The script of your experience is instantaneously being written by every subconscious desire that you withhold from the Light of Truth. It seems to be in time, yet when you look carefully as the Light of Truth you will see that no script is being written at all.

The desire to see your bother as not awake is the same as your desire not to see yourself as awake. This is the desire for a story on a timeline.

Your desire to see your brother as imperfect or limited is the same as your desire to see yourself as imperfect. This is the desire for a story on a timeline.

The desire to feel superior is the same as the desire to feel inferior and deny that you are as God made you. These are shadows the Son of God casts in his holy mind.

Love knows not of because, or if then, or when, wherefore or whys. Nor story. No story tells you who you are. The ego is always looking for a story that will make "you" feel better. This is in the play of trading illusions: shadow puppet battles between thoughts that mean nothing, shopping in time for the experience of death, hungering for an opportunity to have an opinion. An opinion is a story, a story of denial

Honesty of God is admission of Divinity, admitting the denials of Divinity, and the refusal to accept what the ego has made as true.

of the Father. Come quickly into the circle of Light–ever shining. Sit quietly in contemplation of the Light, the Light given to you by the Father. See that denials do not exist here. See that peace is here and all the Love that seeking aimlessly in form can never provide. Here Love offers no opinion. It is. Here Love rests in magnitude celebrating only Itself as it is. Honesty is essential–without honesty there is no opportunity to see the truth, as the ego is self delusion. This is not the honesty of the world. The world's honesty is the belief that an exchange of information as the ego sees it is truth. Honesty of God is admission of Divinity, admitting the denials of Divinity, and the refusal to accept what the ego has made as true. Honesty is admitting you have all the power granted you by the Father and ceasing to deny what is granted. Honesty does not come through expressing emotions and feelings. Honesty comes from inner looking at what is true. Does Divine Being–the Light within–recognize what is moving? No, it does not, thus everything that is moving is untrue. Is anything other then perfect peace true? No. Can anything other than perfect peace be known in the Light of Truth? No. This is honesty and simplicity. Honesty is admitting that you are not at peace and thus denying Divinity and choosing again. Choosing is merely ceasing to deny. Heaven does not know what choice is. There is no choice to be Divine. It is denial of Divinity that generates an idea that there is choice and something to choose between. Honesty knows there is no such thing as choice, because choice is two and there is only One.

Miracles are merely expressions of Love, expressions of Christ consciousness that point beyond form, to the formless, to the power of Infinite Being that is untouched by the laws of this world. The laws of this world are concepts and this is beyond concepts. Miracles are a re-appropriation of false creation to point to truth. They arise in consciousness, without changing what is always true, no miracles are needed for what is holy and complete, Infinite Being. You.

Miracles require conviction as it is your conviction in your value of your Self as whole and complete, even though you deny it. This conviction is necessary, this is faith, and faith always points back to your Self. The faithless are lost, because they do not have conviction, conviction that they have more value than they currently perceive. Thus miracles honor your Self. Conviction is an expression of faith in your Self. It denies weakness, which you must do for yourself. Willingness is thus an expression of acceptance of the power you have to always see what is true to you. Ultimately it points to what you must recognize, the power that is always within being to command as the Father commands, thus it is by your command to suffer or end all suffering as you experience it. To admit you can only experience what you desire. However, you cannot command in truth to be separate from Him, nor apart from His Will, thus you must return to Him in your rightful place as a part of Him, unchanged by your desire to experience hell in time.

Mind training is a function in consciousness, the ability to notice objects as well as what is beyond all objects. This is repurposed to notice what is not natural to you, time and objective experience and to see the contrast between time and the timeless nature of who you are. It is a refinement in consciousness to recognize the denial of wholeness, the desire to fragment consciousness for an experience of limitation. Miracles are expressions of consciousness conceived in love, which collapse denial. Denials in reality do not exist. So they are in a sense a play within consciousness, until it is seen that consciousness can never be divided, it is only an idea that it can be divided, and ultimately consciousness does not exist at all.

Honesty is admitting you have
all the power granted you by the Father
and ceasing to deny what is granted.

NASA/ESA and The Hubble Heritage Team

CHAPTER 15

DIVINE PROVIDENCE

The greatest power is to follow the Divine Light within, to see that you are this Light and that nothing of this world changes your true identity. You are always under the authority of God, as you cannot be apart from Him, as much as you desire an experience otherwise. Thus you are an expression of Him and as such you are Divine Providence, given by what is holy to be holy and only that. Your function is the recognition of completion, that you are complete, holy and whole. This means giving all to all as you are given all by the Father. Giving all to all means following the Holy Spirit, the inner Light within, as this is an expression of Divine nature, and to cease the denials that you are already a holy Son of God. I may ask you to give away all you have to the poor, if this is in service to the recognition of Divinity, in service to what you have asked, to know only your Divine nature. It is not to be assumed; however, that this is automatic. Divinity is available now and has no conditions in its recognition–it is not waiting for you to give away objects for you to see what is already here. If you give away all your money, as many have, as an attempt to win Heaven in the belief that sacrifice is salvation, this is not in service to the whole. Eons

You are Divine Being and as such automatically carried by the grace of God, regardless of your seeming situation in the world.

of monks, priests, friars, nuns and sadduhs have taken this path, looking at my life as an example and assumption of seeming poverty as the path to God. Giving away things in form does not ensure salvation as long one thought is maintained of judgment. Being poor can have an identity all its own, the pride of seemingly having nothing. Give all to all does not automatically mean give all things in form away. Judgment is poverty of Spirit, which is of far greater concern. Give everything away to the poor and follow me emphasizes the follow me and helps you discover where your treasure is. Give all to all is to follow me in Guidance, without question. Christ control is the only means of true salvation. It is to see what you have given away of your natural inheritance from the Father, forgive yourself what never happened and see no error. It may be given that it is most helpful to give what seem to be objects away, so you can see ultimately they are meaningless to you since you created them. You will find a great lightness in this and in many cases objects just fall away in importance naturally with your willingness to recognize what is already here. The joy of your true nature so far extends beyond any idea you have ever had that an object can bring you happiness and in this you will no longer wish to continue to pretend it is possible to own anything when you are everything.

It is by far the greatest value to look with me at every belief and desired experience for objects of the world, the beliefs you hold about objects of the world providing safety and comfort, thus all of the ways you hold onto objects to support a sense of personal identity–all the desire to seemingly have or not have objects in this world, rather than be who you are. You will see that objects hold neither dominion nor necessity for you. Know that objects, such as the concept of money and ownership, are being clutched tightly by the dead. You made them as an attempt to deny your natural inheritance and thus these concepts weigh heavily on your holy mind. In the misuse of your divine power you can manifest an unlimited number of seeming objects and keep the identity of death. When you see that you are Life itself, and have miscreated all of this insanity, what need will you have for another object? Give all that you think you own to my care and guidance to use in purpose of seeing what is true. It is always about guidance for what is most helpful and not to deny what I ask, because what I ask of you is always on behalf of your deepest desire to know who you are and see that true happiness is only this. You are Divine Being and as such automatically carried by the grace of God, regardless of your seeming situation in the world.

Would it not be easier then
just to accept who you are?
To celebrate that you are not
some weak perishable object
subject to the sands of time?
NASA, ESA

CHAPTER 16

ACCEPTANCE OF LIGHT

Infinite Light is always calling you home–to see that you are home. No expectations, nothing to do or change. *I need do nothing.* Yet the ego is always doing something that is nothing. This is a burial ground, pretending that life is form. Pretending that you have some function in form. You are beyond form. Now it is time to look before form began. All the blessings before form began, before the tiny mad idea. Before the objection to timeless Infinite Being, pretending not to be itself as it is, perfect, whole and complete. Pretending not to be of the Father, insisting it is not of the Father. How can this be? Insisting you are not of God, when there is only God.

You believe in time, yet you never question, what is time? Is this known or is this an idea? You believe in death, yet you do not question, what is death?

You desire endings and beginnings. You love these experiences, more than being as you are, already total Love. You want to love and hate experience–make an experience and then hate it to deny that you made it. The wheel of Samsara, suffer more and blame God, yet you want this experience. To be a victim and to be a victimizer in endless cycles, a vast wasteland of repeating cycles of denying true identity. All experience to deny peace is already here. All experiences to swear that God has stolen eternal life from you and leaves you damned. Determined to protect the darkest and deepest corners of your mind knowing it cannot bring you happiness, yet determined to experience it all. Because you know that you cannot die. Yet you suffer, complain and toil, resentful for what you have made. Beloved, there is only all in, for what you withhold from the Light of Truth you only withhold from yourself. You are the Kingdom of Heaven, unless you deny that you are. I have offered a means to quickly see that you have all the power granted to you by Heaven to drop the chains and take your rightful place–yet you must not hold back, because if you do, you are agreeing that you are weak, that what you have created can harm you–you are agreeing with your own delusions. This is a collaboration with what cannot be, kicking and yelling that you will be punished, denied, all when it is only up to you. It has only all been up to you to look carefully before time began to see that time cannot be without you. Time may seem to change but it cannot change without you. Time cannot be known without the timeless. What is relative cannot be known without what is beyond relative. Would it not be easier then just to accept who you are? To celebrate that you are not some weak perishable object subject to the sands of time? Infinite Light as it is, everything pure and reflecting the magnificence of all the Love the Father has bestowed upon you.

Infinite Light as it is, everything pure
and reflecting the magnificence
of all the Love the Father
has bestowed upon you.

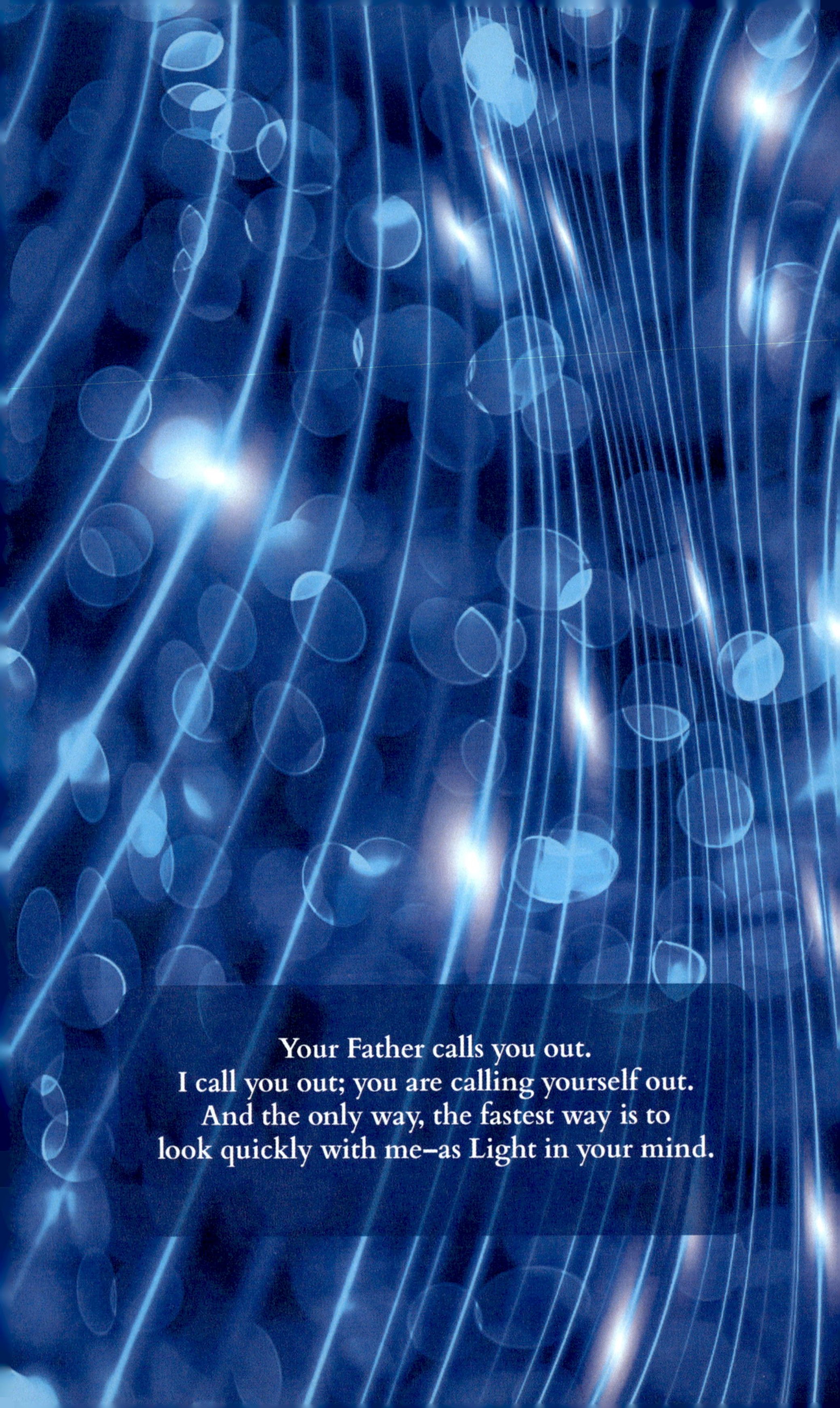
Your Father calls you out.
I call you out; you are calling yourself out.
And the only way, the fastest way is to
look quickly with me–as Light in your mind.

CHAPTER 17

DESIRE TO EXPERIENCE PAIN

Every thought believed is a delay. When you delay looking you delay the celebration that is always available to you. You deprive yourself your daily bread, as given by the Father. Infinite happiness is always yours. This you would delay in time, when all is available to you in eternity. Pain is an idea that you enjoy and revel in as experience, while claiming you do not know it. This is Face of Innocence, the denial that you do have the power to both create suffering and dispel it from your holy mind. It is very simple. Cease to deny what is already yours, what no pain, suffering, anger, or hatred can hide from you, unless you choose it to seem to be so. There is neither future nor past, unless you choose for it to seem to be so in your experience. This is where you learn what you are choosing for, for you can see that you have been choosing against what is most holy and natural to you, all that is given by the Father, Infinite Love. This course is really about all or nothing. There is no midpoint at which Divine nature and the idea you have created of yourself meet. There is no negotiation, as is common in the ways of the world.

The ego negotiates, the Father does not. Negotiation is the idea of win and loss. Heaven can not negotiate with what never happened. Yet you still have the desire to negotiate–to have heaven and hell meet in the mid line. Half of one is still hell. The tiniest compromise is hell, even though you believe the ego that some small part of a personal identity can be preserved and you can still yet find Heaven within. You believe that some safety and protection lies in hell, and thus you would hold yourself, and your brother with you, in a bin of suffering and despair. Do not underestimate the rage that is hidden in this bin of suffering, even the smallest

It is very simple. Cease to deny what is already yours, what no pain, suffering, anger, or hatred can hide from you, unless you choose it to seem to be so.

attempt to hold on to some part of an identity that is never given by the Father. It requires rage to pretend that you and your Father are not One. You have cast yourself into hell by your desire to have an experience–a dream of pain and suffering. Your Father calls you out. I call you out; you are calling yourself out. And the only way, the fastest way is to look quickly with me–as Light in your mind. Let no corner be denied this Light or you will continue to find hell–secret patches cropping up on a timeline that convince you that only death can be your reward. You are convinced that death is your just reward for denying your Father, and I tell you now it is not. You seek vengeance as experience for yourself, when your Father has no idea that such a thing as vengeance exists. You do not know it either, and thus you must dream it, to pretend that it exists and experience it as though it does exist through a world and your brother. Yet if you allow him, your brother as your Father brings you glad tidings of happiness–a reminder of the eternal Light within. Thus to see the Light in your brother is to see the Light that shines within you, only this. You cannot take this journey without your brother because your brother is you–an expression of yourself. And how you choose to see him, is how you choose to see and experience yourself. If you see him limited, so shall you see yourself ever limited. If you see him in hatred so you will see yourself in hatred. If you see him in pain so you worship at pain's table within yourself. He merely reflects the world of heaven or hell experience you have miscreated for yourself. Every stone you cast out against your brother never goes out, it merely rests in eternal suffering as a shadow in your holy mind, convincing you that you are surely damned.

Pain is simply the means by which you attempt to deny who you are. It is a refusal to let go of body identity. You would rather be in pain than rejoice in who you are. You cannot be without pain until you see through your desire for it as valuable. Pain is unnatural to you and does not appear without your desire to experience it. Pain is a memory that cannot be known in timelessness. It is a desire to experience a past, and is thus time bound; a desire to make the past real. Pain is an attempt to block my voice– your voice for Truth. The voice that reminds you that who you are does not know what pain is. Today we will look at the insanity of how you actually relish the experience of pain, and then create an experience in which you do not recall that you relish the experience of it, and thus maintain a sense of what is not natural to you. When you admit this you can also see how you can transcend the experience of it. The true power you have as granted by the Father, a power that does not invest in the experience of pain, as it is all that is. On the cross I did not experience pain because I did not desire to experience it, in admitting full unity with the Father, pain is impossible. In seeing all as the same, as the Father sees it, all as the same–Love only–pain cannot coexist with perfect Love. Desire expresses as rage which hides itself in a diversity of expressions within consciousness. Make no mistake that this is all the same, a denial of Infinite Love, infinite perfection. Pain is a judgment against yourself that the Father does not share. Pain is at your command to keep or to cease. See that you provide all the power that makes pain seem real, an investment in what can never be natural to your holiness.

Every thought believed is a delay.
When you delay looking you delay
the celebration that is always available to you.
You deprive yourself your daily bread,
as given by the Father.
Infinite happiness is always yours.

To trust what is beyond the idea
of a personal identity brings the mind
back to its original state of being.
NASA, ESA, STScI

CHAPTER 18

TRUST

Trust is completely unknown to you in your natural state. Infinite Love is all that is and thus does not know what trust is. Yet in the world of form, in the belief that form exists, trust points back to your Self. Trust cannot move out from you to objects or circumstances, although you believe it does. The need for trust takes belief; a belief that things are not exactly as they are, as they are given by the Father to His holy Son, Divine perfection, whole and unchanged by time and space. The ego does not know trust, for the ego made the need for trust to deny what is already whole and beyond trust.

Thus trust is a helpful concept when those with a belief that there is something less than wholeness must look beyond this idea that wholeness is not already here to find him Self. In this case, trust is necessary to find what is beyond the idea that trust exists. To trust what is beyond the idea of a personal identity brings the mind back to its original state of being. This is why trust and faith settle every problem now. Trust is not about a future experience of being safe. This is an idea of the ego. Trust is accepting Divinity now, until it is seen that there is no trust needed to be Divine Being, what is already here.

No one can awaken from this world without full trust, for untrusting is siding with a sense of limitation and lack. It is an agreement–a desired experience–that something or someone is untrustable and thus unworthy of trust. And we have already discussed that unworthiness is not of the Father. Unworthiness is of the wrong mind and a desired experience to feel unworthy of Love. Not trusting is merely the desire to experience lack within, an attempt to convince yourself that you are less than you are, perfect as the Father made you. This is why trusting in me is to trust in yourself as God made you. It seems like a step, yet it is acceptance of your Holiness now. Your brother is the representative in your mind that points back to where you do not trust yourself, and find yourself unworthy of all that is given to you by the Father. Your brother is the means given by which you recognize your holiness–or the desire to deny it. Thus full faith in your brother is necessary, just as faith in me is necessary, as this is trusting yourself–Divinity as given in wholeness from the Father. This is why it is necessary to look carefully at the desire to not see your brother fully as yourself. When you do, you will see that you do indeed reject him and that this is a desired experience of rejecting yourself, denying the peace of Heaven from yourself now.

Acceptance is of great value in the reversal of the desire to deny yourself. Infinite Love in the absolute sense does not know acceptance or rejection because it is, and thus you, in your natural state, do not know acceptance either. I have used the words *the Holy Spirit accepts* and the *ego rejects* only to point you toward yourself. I can assure you that Divinity knows neither acceptance nor rejection. It is What Is. The wrong mind miscreates the world through rejection of holiness, thus the reversal is offered through the term acceptance to point back to the real world–ultimate reality of What Is–through acceptance as a means of recognizing and honoring what is already here. The ego interprets acceptance as accepting things as less than they are–a sad sacrifice, the idea that suffering must be accepted. Emotions must be accepted. Pain and guilt must be accepted. This form of acceptance has nothing to do with you as Divine Being. This is rejecting Divine Grace under the disguise of acceptance. This is accepting less than who you are and thus rejection of Divine Being. How can this bring peace of mind? This is not integrity that is given by Love through the Holy Spirit. Integrity of Spirit is to see what is true, that these movements are not to be accepted as what is happening, they are to be seen as false–untrue in the Light of Divine Being. This is the means by which you accept–honor–your power as Divine Being as given in holiness by the Father.

True acceptance is accepting who you are and accepting that if you are not perfectly at peace, then you are misusing creative power to have an experience that is not peace. This is Honesty of God–honesty that honors your Father and thus yourself, all that is given by Love to celebrate Love as it is, whole and complete. Acceptance of God is to cease to deny yourself as Love. This is trusting that the idea you have of yourself is unreal and does not exist, the recognition that the play of feeling limited and weak has no value to you. Trusting in this manner is to release yourself from the self-imposed chains that do not exist, to see in reality you do not want them. This is the means to step beyond trust into all the power God has given you as His holy Son.

The denial is the need for healing.
This is the only thing that must be healed,
the denial of Infinite Love.
European Space Agency and Wolfram Freudling (Space Tele
Coordinating Facility/European Southern Observatory, German

CHAPTER 19

HEALING

Healing is a thought. Like forgiveness, it is a helpful thought until it is seen that there is no one to heal and no one who is healing. There is only Love, yet forgiveness is given as the remedy to the belief that error of thought, and thus sin, is real. And to those who believe that sin is real, and that the only justice is punishment for sin, a justice that is not of the Father, forgiveness is the remedy that points back to what is beyond healing, to see that the need for healing never happened. Just as the tiny mad idea, the idea that healing is necessary never happened. And so, we look deeply at healing and what healing is, the remedy given to the one who believes it is possible to sleep. This is a sleep without rest. This is the sleep of the dead who claim that God cannot be known, that they are abandoned by the very One who can never abandon them. And in this desire to experience abandonment all the sickness of the world arises. Sickness, suffering and death. The dream of death and destruction, where unhappiness reigns and the body seems to fall ill or with mishaps and pain accepted as the way of life.

This is the way of the ego, the way of death and eternal damnation. Life is who you are, the answer to the question*, I am* *not a body, what am I?* This is the only question that has value in this world, until it is seen that even this question need not be asked, for the answer is self-apparent. Unless it is denied. The denial is the need for healing. This the only thing that must be healed, the denial of Infinite Love. Miracles are not seeming expressions in form. Miracles are natural expressions of Divine nature celebrating itself. Form may reflect miracle mindedness, as form reflects what is in the mind; however, the truly miracle minded make no mistake that appearances in form can in any way define who they are.

As shared in *A Course in Miracles*, healing is of the mind–to see what has been denied and cease to deny it through the means of miracles and forgiveness. This shift in perception reveals that nothing ever happened. The Son of God remains always untouched–shining Holy Light of the Father with the Son as One in Light and One in Truth. Happiness guaranteed. Where in this world is happiness guaranteed?

Some may point to the spontaneous healing that occurred when I touched people of the world as a demonstration of healing that is called for in *A Course in Miracles*. Let me be clear in saying that touching people in this world is not healing. The healing that seemed to occur was a simple ordinary expression of Divinity and alignment with the Father's Will. Thus it seemed to appear in the images in form that the blind could see and the dead walked. It is a reflection of the power of a healed mind. The most helpful point is that in this movement in consciousness I had no illusions that healing was needed or that there was anyone to heal, as there simply is no other to heal. My instruction was to not speak about these appearances, for the Spirit of Truth does not emphasize appearances and changes in appearances. The Spirit of Truth, just as you are, is beyond what appears in form and merely points back to the truth of what is already holy, whole and complete. There is neither appearance in form nor change in form that can prove who you are. Nor define who you are. Form merely points back to who you are. See no error is to see no error in form. To emphasize healing in form in any manner is not the fastest means for the recognition of Divinity. It can be a distraction. Remember, I said not to ask me for help healing the body, rather, to ask me to reveal the underlying conditions for which healing is needed–the beliefs and desires in the subconscious mind that lead to the desired experience that something has gone wrong, and thus that healing is necessary. This is true healing that is in service to the recognition of Divinity.

As soon as the focus devolves to healing form–the desire for changes in form–the real power of the acceptance of Divinity is lost. It is a denial of Divinity cloaked as healing. It is the use of magic, which merely trades one form of belief for another. Without looking at the thoughts below the level of awareness the timeline remains with the attempt to change form and save a body. The emphasis becomes saving a body and reinforces the belief that salvation is saving a body and changing form. You are beyond a body. It is looking at the thoughts with me to see the beliefs and desire for the experience of illness, to see the desire for the experience that there is something to be healed and that there is someone who needs healing. This is what leads to freedom of the mind–the recognition that there is nothing to heal and no one who needs healing. Infinite Love never needs healing, only the wrong mind, which denies that it is already Infinite Love, needs this form of thought reminder to cease the desire to dream of forgetting what it already is.

Carefully contemplate each desire and see that each is a decision to deny who you truly are and that you can never truly deny who you are. This is a valuable use of time to see you are already timeless.

CHAPTER 20

CLEARING BELIEFS AND DESIRES

All of the beliefs of the ego thought system that are below awareness–in the subconscious mind–are given in *A Course in Miracles*. It is suggested to review and quickly clear these beliefs and desires in Light Circle Sessions. This is merely a symbol of reviewing all of these with me in the Light of Truth to see that they have no meaning, other than the meaning you would give them. This is where willingness is acceptance of your true power as One with the Father. Notice in each case how the desired experience is for you to feel more or less than you already are. See that these are desires for objective experience–the experience of an object acted on by the world. Infinite Being does not know more or less. Infinite Being is. Thus is the contrast between what you are and the miscreation to experience what you are not. These beliefs and desires are all the same in that they are denials of Divinity. Many of these desires may seem to be very close or the same, and in the Light of Truth they are the same. Within the ego thought system, to look at each one in the Light of Truth is helpful as this demonstrates the diversity

No thought, feeling, or emotion–no objective experience–arises without the desire for it, and if you believe it, you will seem to experience the effects of your desire.

of ways the decision to experience separation displays as the experience of fragmentation of consciousness below the level of awareness. Carefully contemplate each one and see that each is a decision to deny who you truly are and that you can never truly deny who you are. This is a valuable use of time to see you are already timeless. In each case the beliefs given in *A Course in Miracles* are retranslated to demonstrate the desire for the experience that exists below the belief. No thought, feeling, or emotion–no objective experience–arises without the desire for it, and if you believe it, you will seem to experience the effects of your desire.

Editors Note: All the beliefs in this Chapter from A Course in Miracles *are italicized.*

Four Core Beliefs of the Ego

1. *You believe that what God created can be changed by your own mind.* Thus you desire an experience using your mind to attempt to change what God created perfect and to experience imperfection. You desire an experience of change to deny changelessness.

2. *You believe that what is perfect can be rendered imperfect or lacking.* Thus you desire to experience feeling you are imperfect or lacking to deny divine perfection. You desire an experience of projecting imperfection as a world apart from yourself for the experience of imperfection and lack.

3. *You believe that you can distort the creations of God, including yourself.* Thus you desire an experience where you experience distortions in the creations of God, including yourself.

4. *You believe that you can create yourself, and that the direction of your own creation is up to you.* Thus you desire an experience in which you create yourself and the direction of your own creation is up to you. You desire an experience of directing creation apart from God and thus to feel left homeless by your Creator.

Beliefs and Desires that Miscreate the Experience of Fragmentation in Consciousness.

You believe the correction takes time, thus you desire an experience in which the acceptance of the correction, and thus the atonement, takes time.

You do not believe you are responsible for what you believe. You desire an experience where you do not feel responsible for what you believe. Professed ignorance over miscreation is never bliss, it is always hell.

You believe that if you were to look at all the beliefs and desires below your level of awareness you would be destroyed by God. Thus you desire an experience where you are afraid to look at all the beliefs and desires below your level of awareness and that you will be destroyed by God if you do. This is the means by which the desire to experience separation from your Creator is maintained–to miscreate fear around directly looking at denials. See that in the Light of Infinite Being you do not know fear and separation from your Creator is impossible.

You believe you cannot dispel any belief. You desire an experience where you feel that you do not have the power to dispel beliefs. This is a means by which you delay acceptance of Divinity. It is the same as the belief in an order of difficulty in miracles. You desire an experience of an order of difficulty in miracles, and thus hold yourself bound in time.

You believe God can be killed. You desire an experience of killing God.

You believe you can be killed. You desire an experience of being killed. You desire an experience of blaming God for killing you, when God, your true nature, does not know what killing is.

You believe your brother can be killed. You desire an experience of your brother being killed. You desire an experience of killing and being killed.

You believe that what your physical eyes do not see does not exist. Thus you desire an experience of denying what your physical eyes do not see.

You believe you can order your thoughts and that the order of your thoughts is up to you. You desire an experience of ordering your thoughts, where ordering your thoughts has more value to you than your Identity, which has no thoughts other than the thought of God. Thus you desire to experience the effects of ordering your thoughts, where you feel some thoughts have more value than other thoughts. You desire to feel lost in thoughts. This is the fundamental desire to experience Cause as separate from Effect.

You believe that what you think is ineffectual and has no impact on what you experience. Thus you desire an experience of feeling the impact of your thoughts and not recognizing that you miscreated them.

You believe that God holds your evil deeds against you. Thus you desire an experience where you feel that what you do is evil and that God will punish you because of them. This is the same as your desire for an experience of attack–the desire to experience holding sin, what never happened–against yourself.

You believe you are being punished by God. You desire an experience where you feel punished by God. You desire an experience of punishing yourself.

You believe God seeks vengeance. You desire to have an experience of fearing the vengeance of God and vengeance upon yourself and others.

You believe this journey with the Holy Spirit is sacrifice. Thus you desire to have an experience of feeling sacrifice in following the Holy Spirit. Sacrifice is guilt, the idea that guilt is true. It is the desire to keep guilt to deny the recognition of Divine nature. Since following the Holy Spirit is the expression of Divinity, to not follow the Holy Spirit is attack upon yourself.

You believe that God rejects you. You desire an experience of feeling rejected by God and then feeling angry about it. You desire an experience of rejecting yourself and then feeling angry about it. You desire an experience of rejecting God. You desire an experience of rejecting your brother. See that these desires are all the same, the desire to reject Love and experience it as apart from you. Anger is casting yourself out of Heaven through projection, the desire to prove that you are outside of Heaven–outside of yourself.

In each case the beliefs given in A Course in Miracles are retranslated to demonstrate the desire for the experience that exists below the belief.

You believe that lack is possible. You desire an experience of feeling lack and that something is lacking. See that the ego thought system applies lack indiscriminately to objects, events, your brother and to God–all ideas that you have about yourself as lacking, while it is the desire to experience limitation.

You believe others are fighting you for authorship through what they say. You desire an experience where you feel others are fighting you for authorship through what they say.

You believe you can usurp the power of God. You desire an experience where you feel you can usurp the power of God and thus feel you are unholy. See that this is the desire to usurp Divine power as given by the Father. How can you usurp what you already are?

You believe you create your reality. You desire an experience where you feel you create your own reality, a reality separate from your Creator.

You believe that your creation was anonymous, meaning you believe your creation is without Source. Thus you desire an experience of creating and experiencing the impossible–that you are without Source. The ego is without source as it is unreal. This is the desire to experience the unreal.

You believe you can author yourself. You desire an experience of authoring yourself, an authorship apart from your Creator. This is the desire to deny that you are authored by God and thus One with Him.

You believe in time. You desire an experience of time through denying you are one with your Creator. You desire an experience in which you deny you are timeless.

You doubt you exist at all. You desire an experience in which you doubt you exist at all. This is a helpful doubt indeed, if you use it to doubt the existence of the ego.

You believe what you do or do not do has an impact on you. You desire an experience of feeling that what you do or do not do has an impact on you.

You believe that what others do has an impact on you. Thus you desire an experience that what others do or do not do has an impact on you. This is a means by which you deny yourself Love, which is being. The doer and the one being done to are the same, denial of being what you are.

You believe that what you say has an impact on you. Thus you desire an experience of what you say having an impact on you.

You believe it is possible to reject someone else or something happening in the world. Thus you desire an experience of rejection. Since all is One, you desire an experience of rejecting God and yourself.

You desire an experience of feeling there is something wrong in the world.

You desire an experience of feeling there is something wrong with you.

You desire an experience of feeling there is something wrong with others.

You believe that your desire to reject is your salvation. Thus you desire experiencing rejection as a means of salvation. This is a means to deny yourself the recognition of true salvation and that you are already saved, as Life given by the Father.

You believe that rejecting yourself and Divine nature, the Holy Spirit, is your salvation. You desire an experience of rejecting yourself as a means to deny yourself true salvation.

You believe you are the author of yourself and others. Thus you desire an experience where you author yourself and others, and deny Authorship by the Father.

You are very fearful of everything you have perceived but have refused to accept. You desire an experience of being fearful of what you perceive and have refused to accept as your own miscreation.

You believe that because you have refused to accept it, you have lost control over it. You desire an experience where you create perception and refuse to accept it, so that you have an experience of losing control over what you perceive.

You believe you need to do something to feel whole or complete. You desire an experience where you feel you need to do something to feel whole and complete.

You believe you are an image of your own making. You desire an experience where you feel you are an image of your own making, and thus deny the image of the Father that you are.

You believe you are separated from your source. You desire an experience where you feel separate from your source and to feel angry about it.

You believe that death is possible. You desire an experience of death. You desire an ongoing experience of death of holiness as a means of salvation. You desire an experience of death of a body as a means of salvation.

You believe that peace comes after death. You desire an experience where you feel that no peace can be found until after the death of the body, yet death is occurring in every moment the Light is denied. You desire an experience where you can find no peace in the present moment and that you must die to find it. When you choose experience through desire, the denial of who you are, you are dead now. You desire an experience of trying to find peace in the future, through death, without ever finding it.

You believe your salvation lies in the death of a body. You desire an experience of trying to find salvation through death of a body without ever finding salvation.

You believe you are unworthy of Life–of being synonymous with God. You desire an experience of feeling unworthy of being synonymous with God. You desire an experience of feeling unworthy of your Self.

You believe darkness exists. You desire an experience of darkness.

You believe that if you allow no change to enter into the ego you will find peace. You desire an experience of attempting to stop change entering the ego to find peace while actually denying the peace that you are in your natural state.

You believe that projecting the ego's thought system is valuable. You desire an experience of projecting the ego's thought system and feeling it is valuable, more valuable than Divine Being.

You believe your worth is established by teaching or learning. Thus you desire an experience where you feel you gain if you teach or lose if you do not teach. You desire an experience of gaining if you learn and losing if you do not feel you learn. Yet as spirit you need know nothing nor teach anything to be who you are. Thus this is the value of unlearning everything you think you know or what you must learn and being what you learn is true. Expression of Divinity is everything

Since following the Holy Spirit is the expression of Divinity, to not follow the Holy Spirit is attack upon yourself.

and thus teaches nothing. The demonstration of recognizing who you are is divine expression as it is, whole and complete.

You believe it is possible to be superior to others. Thus you desire an experience of feeling you are superior to others and feeling pleasure in it, yet since pain and pleasure are the same, this is also a pain that makes you feel alienated from your brother, your Father and your Self.

You believe others can be superior to you. You desire an experience where you feel others are superior to you and then feeling fearful and angry about it.

You believe what you do or say has an effect on others. You desire to miscreate an experience of feeling what you say or do has an effect on others and thus feeling pleasure when they seem to respond as you wish or pain when they do not. There is only One, Cause and Effect are One. Divine being does not know an other or an effect on an other.

You believe that what you do or say has an effect on you. You desire to miscreate an experience that what you say or do has an effect on you. If you like what you say or do, you feel pleasure, if you do not like what you say or do, you feel pain.

You believe the ego exists. You desire an experience of having an ego and the effects of the idea that it is real. Thus you desire to experience all the effects of the miscreation of an ego thought system.

You believe that fear is real. You desire to miscreate an experience of fear.

You believe pain is real. Pain is merely an expression of the denial of Divinity and the desire to hold on to personal identity–to project experience outside of yourself. Thus you desire an experience of pain.

You believe you can be separate from your true reality. You desire an experience of being separate from your true reality.

You believe your origin is open to belief. You desire an experience where your origin is open to belief.

You do not believe there is another way of perceiving. You desire to miscreate an experience where you have forgotten there is another way of perceiving and thus place true perception out of your awareness.

You give only because you believe you are somehow getting something better. You desire to miscreate an experience where you give with the expectation you will somehow be getting something better.

You believe you must give to get. You desire an experience where you experience giving as essential to getting.

You believe in scarcity. You desire to experience scarcity.

You believe I am mistaken in choosing you. You desire an experience of feeling I am mistaken in choosing you. You desire an experience of denying that you have chosen me to help you. You desire an experience where you deny that the help of the Father is always available to you.

You believe you are here in this world. You desire an experience of being here in this world, apart from the Father.

You believe that you must escape from the ego. You desire an experience of attempting to escape the ego while denying you miscreated it and claiming that you are powerless to escape it. You desire the experience of an ego Satan–and the experience of doing battle with it to attempt to win salvation. You desire the experience of doing battle with another, when no other exists.

You want to believe you are separate. You desire an experience of feeling you are separate.

You believe that strife is possible. You desire to miscreate an experience of feeling strife is possible.

You believe it is possible to attack God. You desire an experience of attacking God. Thus you desire to have an experience of feeling attacked since you are synonymous with God.

You believe God will retaliate against you. You desire to miscreate an experience of feeling God will retaliate against you.

You believe that the world can retaliate against you. You desire an experience in which the world seems to retaliate against you.

You believe you can think apart from God. You desire an experience in which you feel you can think apart from God.

You believe you order your own thoughts. You desire an experience in which you order your own thoughts and thus experience the effects of the ordering.

You believe God judges against you and that you will be found guilty. You desire an experience of God judging against you and being found guilty. Since you are synonymous with God, you desire to miscreate an experience where you judge yourself and find yourself guilty. Since you are synonymous with your brother, you desire to miscreate an experience of judging your brother and finding your brother guilty. This is the means by which you miscreate the experience of a world of other outside of yourself.

You believe if you appeal for truth that you will be judged against. You desire to miscreate an experience that if you appeal for truth you fear you will be judged against. Yet this is the means by which you judge yourself and find yourself guilty.

You believe you are unworthy of God's love. You desire an experience where you feel unworthy of God's love.

You believe it is possible to attack God. You desire an experience where you feel it is possible to attack God. You believe it is possible to attack yourself. Since you are synonymous with God, in order to continue to feel separate you desire an experience of attacking yourself. You believe it is possible to attack another. Since there is no other, you desire an experience of attacking your brother to maintain the sense of separation. Your brother is synonymous with God, as are you, thus the only way for you to experience attack is to desire it, since there is no other.

You believe it is possible for you to be attacked. Thus you desire an experience of being attacked, and thus miscreating fear that you will be attacked.

You believe that attack is justified. You desire an experience where you feel attack is justified. The expression of the justification of attack is anger. Yet attack does not attack an other, since there is no other. It is an attack upon yourself to preserve a sense of separation from your Creator.

Pain is merely an expression of the denial of Divinity and the desire to hold on to personal identity– to project experience outside of yourself.

You believe you are in no way responsible for attack. You desire an experience of attacking, while experiencing that you are in no way responsible for the miscreation of attack. This is face of innocence. You desire an experience of face of innocence to deny that you are already innocent. You miscreate the experience of guilt while claiming that you are not miscreating it, rather than be who you already are–pure, innocent, and complete.

You believe attack is salvation, thus you desire an experience of attack as a means for salvation.

You believe retaliation is possible. You desire an experience of being retaliated against. You desire an experience of retaliating against others.

You believe that you can think apart from God. You desire an experience of thinking apart from God and experiencing the effects–fear and desolation–of thinking apart from God.

You believe that what you think has value. You desire an experience that what you think has value, more value than the Infinite nature of being and thoughts of God.

You believe what you think has more value than the thoughts of others. You desire an experience in which what you think has more value than the thoughts of others and experience pride in this. Pride is the desire for the experience of unhappiness.

You believe that the thoughts of others are more important than your thoughts. You desire an experience where the thoughts of others feel more important than your thoughts, and to feel deprived and limited by this feeling. You believe more thoughts will solve this condition, where the solution can never be found in thought. The only solution is ceasing to deny true identity.

You believe that what is destructible is real and that it justifies anger. Thus you desire an experience where you perceive what is destructible is real and that anger can be justified to protect the sense of personal identity separate from the Father.

You believe anger is justified. You desire an experience of feeling anger is justified. You believe anger is justified to prove that God has taken something from you, yet you use anger to deny that God has given you everything.

You believe you can be persecuted. You desire an experience of being persecuted.

You believe the world was made to persecute you. You desire an experience of the world persecuting you.

You believe being persecuted is helpful. You believe persecution is the path to freedom and thus experience persecution as valuable, even while you suffer the miscreation of it.

You believe it is acceptable to follow the ego thought system. You believe projection is helpful as a path to salvation. You desire an experience of following the ego thought system through projection and condemnation as a means to salvation, and thus desire to experience these effects even though salvation can never be found in effects separate from the Father.

You do not believe that blessing your brother is valuable. You desire an experience where blessing your brother has no value, thus you experience no blessings for yourself, as you are One. You believe that if you bless every brother you will be damned. Thus you desire an experience where blessing every brother is perceived to be damnation.

You believe you are without Love. You desire an experience of perceiving you are without Love.

You believe you are without the Kingdom of Heaven. Thus you desire an experience of being without the Kingdom of Heaven.

You believe that you have no access to the Kingdom of Heaven. You desire an experience where you feel you have no access to the Kingdom of Heaven.

You believe the Kingdom of Heaven is denied to you. You desire an experience where you feel the Kingdom of Heaven is denied to you.

You believe you are barred from the Kingdom of Heaven. You desire an experience of feeling barred from the Kingdom of Heaven.

**You desire to miscreate an experience
where you have forgotten
there is another way of perceiving
and thus place true perception
out of your awareness.**

You believe it takes time to recognize the Kingdom of Heaven. You desire an experience where it takes time to experience the Kingdom of Heaven.

You believe that you are separate and outside the Mind of God. You believe that the impossible–being outside the mind of God–is possible. You desire an experience of being outside the mind of God.

You believe that having is the opposite of giving. You desire an experience of having in opposition to giving.

You believe that having rests on getting. You desire an experience that in order to have something you must get something.

You believe there is value in the ego thought system. You desire an experience in which you value the experience of the ego thought system.

You believe that something happening in form defines you. You desire an experience of what seems to be happening in form defining you.

You believe you can attend to what is not true (the ego). You desire an experience where you attend to what is not true (the ego).

You believe you have a choice to be separate from God. You desire an experience of having the choice to have an experience that feels separate from God.

You believe that choice is real. You desire an experience of choice as real.

You believe questions are valuable. You desire an experience of questioning your identity.

You believe there is an order of difficulty in miracles. You desire an experience in order of difficulty in miracles. You are already a miracle and that is all there is.

You believe that God does not know. You believe you can create a world in which God does not know you, and you do not know God the Father. Thus you desire to experience what God does not know. Since you are in essence the same as the Father, you desire an experience in which you do not know. This is the desire for an experience in which you do not know who you are.

You believe your brother is attacking you to tear the Kingdom of Heaven from you. You desire an experience of feeling your brother is attacking you to tear the Kingdom of Heaven from you.

You believe it is better to project than face the insane belief that you have been treacherous to your Creator. You desire an experience of projecting and experiencing that you have been treacherous to your Creator. You desire an experience of projecting rather than seeing that you can never be treacherous to your Creator as you are One with Him.

You believe that your brothers are out to take God from you. You desire an experience of your brother taking God from you to deny that you have taken God from yourself.

If you choose to separate yourself from God, that is what you will think others are doing to you. You desire an experience in which you feel others are separating you from God to deny that you are choosing to feel separate from God.

Your state of mind and your recognition of what is in it depends on what you believe about your mind. You desire an experience of what you believe about your mind having more power than who you truly are.

Holy Spirit will direct you only so as to avoid pain. You believe that the Holy Spirit directing you will cause pain. Thus you desire an experience in which you feel pain when the Holy

Spirit directs you. You desire an experience of feeling pain as a means to deny the acceptance of Divinity and to deny that following the Holy Spirit and my direction means peace and joy.

You believe you have to go through pain to see who you are. You desire an experience of going through pain to see who you are. This is the confused notion that pain is a means to salvation.

You believe you must feel guilty to gain salvation. You believe guilt is salvation. Thus you desire an experience of feeling guilty in the path to salvation. This is the desire to experience guilt rather than Divine nature. This is the confused notion that guilt is a means to salvation.

You believe it is possible to do the opposite of God's Will. Therefore, you believe that an impossible choice is open to you. You desire an experience of doing the opposite of God's Will and thus experience the effects of it. You desire an experience of an impossible choice. All choice is impossible choice. The only choice is purpose, which is not really a choice, but the only choice of true value as a reminder to cease to chose the experience of the untrue.

You believe the Holy Spirit asks for sacrifice. You desire an experience of sacrifice. You desire an experience of sacrifice when you hear the voice of the Holy Spirit. You desire an experience of sacrifice as a means for salvation.

When you avoid the Holy Spirit's guidance in any way this means you want to be weak. You desire an experience of avoiding guidance and feeling weak.

You believe you have withdrawn your gifts from God. You desire an experience of withdrawing your gifts from God. This is actually the experience of withdrawing all of God's gifts from yourself, as you are One with Him.

You believe the world is trying to strip God from you. You desire an experience of feeling the world is stripping God from you. You desire an experience of the world stripping God from you as a path to salvation.

You believe Jesus is trying to strip the world from you and that it is going to be painful. Thus you desire an experience of Jesus trying to strip the world from you and experiencing pain.

You believe you can do a better job. You desire an experience of attempting to do a better job than God.

You desire an experience of having the choice to have an experience that feels separate from God.

You enjoy projecting the world and then not liking it. Thus you desire an experience of projecting the world and pretending that you do not like it–the desired experience that what is happening in the world is being done to you against your will.

You believe that fear is involuntary, thus you desire an experience in which fear feels involuntary.

You believe shame is necessary for the creation of the world, thus you desire an experience of creating a world and feeling shame for it.

You believe you are affected by expressions which you believe are lack of love. Thus you desire an experience of expressions that appear to be lack of love and to feel affected by them as though somehow love can be limited or lost.

You believe error of thought is true, thus you desire an experience of error of thought as true.

You believe that thoughts of this world can fill a perceived lack. Thus you desire an experience of lack and trying to fill the lack with thoughts of this world.

You believe in separation, thus you have a desire to experience separation.

You believe perception is true, thus you desire an experience of perception.

You believe God is not in communication with you, thus you desire an experience of not being in communication with God.

You believe the world is chaotic, thus you desire an experience of chaos.

Perception is impossible without a belief in more and less. Thus you desire an experience where you perceive more and less. Specifically, you desire an experience of simultaneously feeling more and less than you truly are, which knows neither more nor less. Thus your true identity does not know perception. You desire an experience of false perception to deny who you are.

You believe judgment is possible, thus you desire an experience of judgment, and in this you experience judgment against God, yourself and your brother, all to deny that judgment is impossible.

You believe false perception is true, thus you desire an experience in which false perception feels true and thus true to you.

You believe perception has value. Thus you desire an experience where perception feels more real to you than your true identity, which has no perception and places no value on perception.

You believe you cannot completely know God, thus you desire an experience in which you do not completely know God. Thus you desire an experience in which you do not know yourself.

You believe you are what you believe, thus you desire an experience of being what you believe and thus what you perceive.

You believe I am more powerful than you, thus you desire an experience in which I am more powerful than you. This is helpful for a time, yet it can only be seen that we are the same in timelessness.

You believe you can be changed by the Authority of God. Thus you desire an experience of feeling fearful of being changed by the Authority of God. The Authority of God has made you changeless, so this is impossible. The Authority problem is the desire to experience resentment, resentment is the belief in the lack of control, that control is taken away. Yet you desire an experience of resentment, control and the feeling of lack or loss of control all at the same time. This is the same as the desire to feel unstable and seek unceasingly in form for stability. This is also the desire to experience abject terror in the face of God, yet the experience of terror is the desired experience to deny that you are God. See quickly that the Light, which you are, has no idea what terror is.

You feel embarrassed by love, thus you believe embarrassment is possible and desire an experience of embarrassment. You are embarrassed by your relationship with me, thus you desire to have an experience where you are embarrassed in knowing and following me. This is a denial of yourself, as Love itself.

You desire an experience in which miracles, your natural inheritance, seem difficult.

You desire an experience of being attracted to sin, and thus repeatedly experiencing sin rather than being Divine nature.

You believe you are in a body, thus you desire an experience of being in a body.

You believe in the world that you made, thus you desire an experience of the world you made.

You believe you have a function other than the one God gave you, thus you desire to experience a function other than the one God gave you.

You believe you have two functions, thus you desire an experience where you feel divided.

You believe that the sick things which you have made are your real creations, because you believe that the sick images you perceive are the Sons of God. Thus you desire an experience of what you have made as real creations. You desire perceiving sick images as the Sons of God.

You believe to communicate is to make yourself alone and that by communicating you will be abandoned. Thus you desire an experience where communication makes you feel alone and abandoned. This is the desire to be out of communication with your Self. This is the desired experience of attempting to communicate in this world horizontally and feeling continually misinterpreted and misunderstood and feeling angry about it. Horizontal communication is self abandonment. Expression of Divinity is the only true communication as it is at One with Source and continually in communion with Itself. Love does not know horizontal communication, only expression of all that is.

You believe that to be with a body is companionship, thus you desire an experience of being with another body as companionship and thus would hold your brother and yourself as an image of a body, held by guilt, the image that death is possible for your brother, God and for yourself.

You believe loneliness is solved by guilt, thus you desire an experience of loneliness and attempting to solve it through guilt.

You believe that there is safety in guilt and danger in communication, thus you desire an experience of feeling safety in guilt and danger in communication with your brother and yourself, and thus your Creator. Only communion with your Creator, your Self, is real.

You believe it is possible to be host to the ego or hostage to God. This is the choice you think you have, and the decision you believe that you must make. Thus you desire to experience a choice between host to the ego or hostage to God. Can you not see that this is impossible and that in this experience you will always feel divided from yourself? You can only be host to God, yet you desire to have an experience of being host and thus hostage to the ego, to hold yourself hostage to the idea you have miscreated of yourself.

You believe it is possible to feel resistance to awakening, thus you desire an experience of feeling resistance to awakening as a means to delay recognizing who you are. Resistance is merely a form of attempting to preserve a sense of a future which does not exist. Resistance is futile in that it in no way changes who you already are.

Sacrifice is so essential to your thought system that salvation apart from sacrifice means nothing to you. Your confusion of sacrifice and love is so profound that you cannot conceive of love without sacrifice. Thus you desire an experience in which love itself

When you avoid the Holy Spirit's guidance in any way this means you want to be weak.

and true salvation is sacrifice. You desire an experience in which awakening to true nature, Infinite Love, which knows no sacrifice, is experienced as sacrifice. You desire an experience where all that you are and to be who you are is sacrifice. You desire an experience in which love seems denied to you and love fails you, all while denying it to yourself.

You believe God demands sacrifice and being One with God, you demand sacrifice of yourself and thus experience it as true. Pain and illness of the body is a form of desire for the experience of self sacrifice in an attempt to win false salvation and love. It is the true meaning of guilty pleasure.

As host to the ego, you believe that you can give all your guilt away whenever you want, and thereby purchase peace. Thus you desire an experience of attempting to give guilt away to purchase peace, all the while enjoying the pleasure and pain of the purchase price that denies who you are. It is the true meaning of guilty pleasure. Pain and pleasure is an expression of guilt. A desire to experience guilt yet you believe pain and pleasure can hide guilt from you.

You do not believe that you invited the ego to take residence. Thus you desire an experience of being ignorant of inviting the ego in order to have an experience of forgetting who you are.

You believe the ego has more power than you do. Thus you desire an experience of the ego having more power than you, when you have provided all the power to the illusion that the ego exists.

You believe that love demands sacrifice, and thus desire an experience of love as sacrifice, which makes love seem inseparable from attack and fear. You believe that guilt is the price of love, which must be paid by fear. Thus you desire to experience guilt and fear as the price to be paid for Love, when Love knows not sacrifice, guilt nor fear.

You believe that to step outside of your comfort zone, the comfort zone you have created with the ego, means death. Thus you desire an experience of staying within a comfort zone that is death over the expression of Divinity. Safety and comfort are perceivable, and anything perceivable is death. This is why the Spirit seems to ask of you to step outside your self imposed prison of a comfort zone, to see that you are far more powerful than a comfort zone and that you have created a comfort zone to stay imprisoned from your Self. You are synonymous with Life itself, and the Holy Spirit offers you the only true Comfort. Thus this is the meaning of the statement, *you can do anything I ask,* because you are no different than me. This is the only true comfort, the comfort and infinite joy of honoring the expression of Divinity. Look carefully at the desire to do battle with the Holy Spirit, as this is the desire for the experience of a battle within yourself.

You believe without the ego all would be chaos, thus you desire an experience of maintaining the ego in the false experience of avoiding chaos while actually creating the experience of chaos. This is the desire to be lost in the dream of chaos. Divine nature, the natural state of being, does not understand chaos.

*You believe you must understand it (*Divinity*) or it is not real.* Thus you desire an experience of attempting to understand Divine nature in order to miscreate an experience that Divine nature, what is most natural to you, is unreal. In the Light of Divinity see that this is impossible. Divine nature can only be recognized and accepted as it is, whole and complete.

You believe specialness is heaven and not hell. Thus you desire an experience of feeling special as a path to salvation which is hell–superior to your Self, which is impossible. Thus you desire an experience of specialness to maintain the experience of hell.

The ego is a disagreement about what completion is. Thus you desire an experience of having a disagreement with yourself about what completion is.

When you believe there is a difficulty in order in miracles, you believe truth cannot deal with perceived difficulties only because you would withhold some things from the truth. Thus you desire an experience of withholding some things from the truth and experiencing the effects of withholding truth from yourself. This is how you deny yourself with the miscreation of order of difficulty in miracles.

Expression of Divinity is the only true communication as it is at One with Source and continually in communion with Itself.

If you believe God cannot enter where God wills to be, you must be interfering with His Will. Thus you desire an experience of God not entering where God Wills to be–an attempt to interfere with His Will to deny His presence is always with you. Thus you desire an experience where you feel you can defy His Will for you for perfect happiness.

If you believe the holy instant is difficult for you, it is because you have become the arbiter of what is possible, and remain unwilling to give place to One Who knows. Thus you desire an experience of the holy instant being difficult for you. The whole belief in orders of difficulty in miracles is centered on this. You desire an experience where you are unwilling to give place to God.

While you believe that your reality or your brother's is bounded by a body, you will believe in sin. While you believe that bodies can unite, you will find guilt attractive and believe that sin is precious. Thus you desire the experience of keeping guilt and sin alive through the joining of bodies. You desire an experience where sin is experienced as precious.

The belief that bodies limit mind leads to a perception of the world in which the proof of separation seems to be everywhere. Thus you desire the experience where the body seems to limit the mind and thus to experience finding proof of separation everywhere through experiences of the body.

You believe bodies can join, thus you desire an experience of bodies joining to deny that the Infinite mind is already joined.

The body does appear to be the symbol of sin while you believe that it can get you what you want. You desire an experience of the body getting you what you want. This can never tell you who you are. While you believe that it can give you pleasure, you will also believe that it can bring you pain. Thus you desire an experience of the body getting what you want so you can experience sin–the experience of pain and pleasure on a timeline.

You believe the body can give you pleasure, thus you desire an experience of pain.

You believe the atonement is murder. Thus you desire to experience murder of yourself rather than the atonement–and ultimately to see there is no need for the atonement whatsoever.

You desire to get rid of peace and keep guilt instead. Thus you desire an experience of guilt to deny yourself peace.

You believe the body is valuable for what it offers. Thus you desire an experience where you feel the body has value in experiencing pleasure and pain and thus manifesting the experience of guilt in a body.

You believe that salvation lies in the body. Thus you desire an experience of attempting to find salvation through a body, rather than seeing in the Light of Truth, this is impossible. Forgiveness is undoing the idea that salvation comes through a body. Salvation is of the mind, the dissolution of the idea of a body.

You believe that peace would dispossess you of guilt and leave you homeless. Thus you desire an experience of finding a home in guilt and the feeling of homelessness in order to avoid peace that is your home.

You believe the world is outside of you and has you in its mercy, thus you desire an experience of the world outside of you having you at its mercy.

You do not believe that the answer of your true identity is already given, thus you desire an experience where you feel the answer is not already given.

You believe that if you look inward, your eyes will light on sin and God will strike you blind. Thus you desire an experience of feeling that if you look inward you will find sin, and God will strike you blind.

You believe you have secrets, thus you desire an experience of keeping secrets, and secrets make you feel apart from God. You use secrets to hide from yourself your Inheritance, thus to deny your Self your daily bread. Secrets are a desired experience to attempt to hide from yourself, as you are always One with God. This is a desire to not know yourself as you are, whole and complete. These are not the same as secrets of this world. This is the secret of hiding true identity from your self, by denying guilt. It is denying that you are denying the Light of Being.

You believe in conflict and that the ego has the power to be victorious. Thus you desire an experience of conflict and feeling that the ego has the power to be victorious.

You believe the body is weak. You desire an experience of weakness in the body. You believe that if the body collapses you will be saved. You believe that if the body experiences illness you will be saved, thus you desire an experience of the body being ill and collapsing to be saved and therefore make you safe from your Divine power. Feeling the body sick gives you pleasure and a sense of power to deny God, guilty pleasure, and look closely to see you desire this experience of guilty pleasure in the body. This is an attempt to falsely join with yourself through the body by making the body real. The body merely expresses what you believe. You have a desire to experience the effects of your beliefs through the body.

For your beliefs converge upon the body, the ego's chosen home, which you believe is yours. You desire an experience in which all that you believe converges on the body–giving the ego a home as though the ego has taken hold of it without your choice. Thus you desire experience in which you deny the ego is your choice, the decision to give it a home as body identification. You have joined with the thought you have made of yourself–the ego–so you can avoid what is already joined in Truth and Light. You desire the experience of the ego joining with the illusion of yourself and keeping the illusion to deny yourself. This is the illusion of losing control of yourself, yet your true Self, the Light within, remains unchanged. Thus you desire the experience of the ego–of suffering and despair and hopelessness, with no way out. See

No thought, feeling, or emotion–no objective experience–arises without the desire for it, and if you believe it, you will seem to experience the effects of your desire.

carefully what you have chosen to experience, and let the memory of the Light–the Holy Spirit within–lead you out. See happily that what you desire to experience is impossible. See in the Light of Divine Being, it is impossible.

You believe life apart from Heaven is possible. You desire an experience where you experience life apart from Heaven as possible, yet this is the same as the desire for an experience of death. The Kingdom of Heaven is within as Life itself, and cannot be apart from you as you are One with the Father in Heaven always.

You believe death is salvation. Thus you desire an experience of death as salvation. You believe you deserve death for denying your Father. Thus you desire an experience of death rather than to know that as a Divine Being of the Father you do not know what death is.

You believe that some injustices are fair and good, and necessary to preserve yourself. Thus you desire an experience where some injustices appear fair and good, thus in this you preserve a sense of identity separate from the Father.

You believe illusions are real, thus you desire to experience illusions as real.

You believe the crucifixion is real. Thus you desire an experience of crucifixion. This desire will lead you to an experience in which you either crucify yourself or your brother, as your brother is yourself, all being one with the Father. And thus you would crucify God, if you could, all for desired experience to deny yourself the Kingdom within that knows not crucifixion.

These are many of the beliefs and thus desired experiences you would hold against your Father and thus deny your Self, being always One with Him. Who with these many desires to deny him Self could ever rest in peace? Would you not give them to me–to the Light of Truth–and find that you eternally rest in the Peace granted you by the Father? In this is a forgiven world without end, amen.

Nothing real can be threatened, nothing unreal exists.

Therein lies the peace of God.

Who with these many desires to deny him Self could ever rest in peace? Would you not give them to me–to the Light of Truth–and find that you eternally rest in the Peace granted you by the Father?

CLARIFICATION OF TERMS

As mentioned in the introduction it is not a requirement to be *A Course in Miracles* (ACIM) student to reflect on this text. It is equally applicable to all students of non duality with the desire to recognize Divine nature. That said, it can be helpful to clarify the meaning of terms from ACIM and *Jesus: A New Covenant ACIM* (ANC ACIM) that appear in the text.

Acceptance, Acceptance of God

> Divine Light accepts all and the ego rejects everything. Yet the ego can pretend to accept emotions, pain, suffering and death as necessary. This is not the acceptance of Divine Light. This is denial–rejection–of Divine Light. Acceptance of the correction–(a change in perception) demonstrates that all thoughts, feelings and emotions are untrue–is immediate. Correction is a change in perception. This is Divine acceptance of the power of Divine Being that is not susceptible to the whims of the untrue.

Thus this means that the untrue need not be accepted as what is happening. Anything that moves or changes can be seen as untrue immediately and as such falls away. This is Acceptance of God–acceptance of Divinity–the real as the only thing that is real. Thus it is not automatically given that any form–thought, feeling, emotion, must be experienced. See that Divine Light does not experience–it merely is. Divine Light has no requirement to experience anything to recognize Divine Light, thus you, as Divine being need not experience anything unless you desire to experience it. All the power is yours to accept that you have denied Divinity and to accept Divinity as all there is. This is the only true acceptance and is merely an admission of what is already here. If you withdraw desire from any experience it will simply disappear as it is a phantom.

Awareness, Light, Infinite Light, Infinite Being

Light is used in many spiritual traditions to refer to the Absolute, Absolute Reality, Abstract Light or God. It is called Awareness and Unborn Awareness or in the case of A Course in Miracles this is called Choiceless Awareness. This is Infinite Love, Love without conditions. Some traditions call this Agape Love. Awareness is unchanging, timeless, and changeless. It is knowledge; however, not the objective knowledge of this world. It is also referred to as What Is. In this book it is also called Light of Being, although it is beyond being. Beingness is the I am presence in which the original God principle shines into the manifest. In the Bible (Aramaic direct translation to English) the reference is John 9: *There is a Light of truth that lights everyone who is born.* The Light–Absolute reality–is unspeakable silence and is before the I am presence. Some traditions refer to Awareness as synonymous with consciousness. Jesus, like Nisargadatta Maharaj, distinguishes consciousness to be different from the Awareness. While manifest cannot be separated in truth from unmanifest, Infinite Light is beyond manifest and unmanifest. Jesus also refers to this as Infinite Mind. It is the quantum field described by quantum mechanics. Only Absolute is real. This is the meaning of the opening statement in *A Course in Miracles: Nothing real can be threatened. Nothing unreal exists. Therein lies the peace of God.* This is true Identity. Indivisible, immutable.

Cause and Effect

In *A Course in Miracles* Jesus shares that in fragmentation in consciousness and thus in the dream of separation the experience is that Cause–God–is separate from Effect, his Son. Since God and the Son of God are the same and thus Cause and Effect are One, this is impossible. Yet, in the world, the play of consciousness and the dream, it appears that one thing can cause another, known as causality. This is the belief that somehow there are objects and that one object can impact another. This generates the experience of duality–more than one–in the dream. Thus in the dream the illusion is that objects in the world act upon a body, and this is the basis for all fear and suffering of the world. This is the basis for the experience of attack, that a body can be attacked, suffer and die.

Communion, True communication, Silence

Communion is a reflection of the natural state of being– communion with Source. It is silence. This is the Source celebrating Itself, as Itself, whole and complete. Communion is pure joy, happiness and peace. It celebrates as what it is. The ego, denial of communion, is the belief that words exchanged between forms is communication and a means to experience communion, when it is a denial that communion with all that is is already here. Love has no reasons, as reasons are a denial of what has no reason to be happiness. Communion and true communication does not happen through words as words are an attempt to deny true communion and communication. Absolute reality–Infinite Light recognizes that no thoughts are real.

Correction

Correction is merely an acceptance that nothing is happening, can happen or has ever happened to change true identity–Divine Light. Accepting the correction means to accept that separation, and thus pain and death, is impossible. Forgiveness is the form of correction and thus change in perception (the false perception that something is happening to a person apart from the whole) that Jesus offers in *A Course in Miracles.*

Creation and Miscreation

God only creates in wholeness and Infinite extension of All that Is celebrating Itself. The world–the dream of separation is miscreation–the misuse of creative potential to miscreate the unreal, the holographic universe–the dream of separation of a world that is both seen and unseen and continually changing. Nothing other than Light is real, thus anything other than Infinite Light is false and a miscreation. Miscreation is a mechanism of consciousness–"creation of what is not real"–the experience of time, change, space, the body, death and thus personal identity and experience that seems apart from the Father–Absolute Reality. Any denial of Divinity–Absolute reality is miscreation.

Crucifixion

Crucifixion is a desired experience arising in the mind of the dreamer. This is the desired experience of self crucifixion– suffering and death for the seeming creation of the world. It is the belief that sin and guilt is real, that the Son of God, in the miscreation of consciousness, somehow engaged in an act of sin against God and thus must be punished for it. This is the symbolic casting out of Adam and Eve from the garden of Eden. Yet God, Infinite Light, does not cast anyone or anything out. God is. Casting out is an idea arising in consciousness, to blame God for what is impossible. Casting out is a desired experience to deny the Light of Divinity through judgment. The crucifixion story of Jesus within consciousness is merely a demonstration that death holds no power over the Son of God, and that all expressions within consciousness are to be seen without exception as expressions of Infinite Love.

Desires

Infinite Light, true nature, is. In Infinite Light desire is unknown. Desires are unnatural energies–investments in the untrue which are hidden in the subconscious mind that maintain the experience of separation and hiding the experience of unity–all is One. Desires are energetic investments in the experience of separation which is carried out by beliefs that deny the Light is our natural state and express in consciousness as objective experiences–the experience of pleasure and pain appearing in the dream which deny that peace is the natural state. Desires miscreate feelings of something more or less, something missing, wanting, feeling inadequate and unworthy. These are all desired experiences to deny the Light of Being. Beliefs below the level of awareness–in the subconscious mind–are a means to attempt to block the recognition of Light–unborn or Choiceless awareness.

Emotions

In *A Course in Miracles* Jesus says that there are only two emotions, Love and fear and that perfect Love casts out fear. Emotions, anything other than a consistent state of joy, love and peace e.g. sadness, anger, frustration, overwhelm, apathy, excitement, are all expressions of desire for experience and are a fear based desire for personal identity and the underlying attempt to prove that beliefs are real. Emotions hide the desire for objective experience as real–the experience of more than one. The demand to express emotions is the demand to keep a part of personal identity intact. As Jesus says in *A New Covenant*, there is no suppression of emotions, see that they do not exist in the Light of Being. Any experience other than the perfect peace of Infinite Divine Light–Love whole and complete expressing joy and perfect happiness in wholeness–is a denial of Divinity. Jesus clearly states that experiencing emotions is not necessary on the spiritual journey, only to recognize quickly that there is an underlying belief that denies Infinite Light and to quickly see all objective experience in the Light of Truth–that it does not exist. This is what Jesus means when he says in the Course, *let us join quickly in an instant of Light*, immediate transcendence of emotions through the power of mind. Happiness, joy and peace are being, What is. This is all there is.

Forgiveness

Forgiveness is the means in ACIM of willingness to see what is true in the Light of Truth. It is a change in perception, a miracle that comes from seeing through a belief as untrue. Beliefs are a mechanism used in consciousness to attempt to place a limitation on Love and thus to deny the recognition of Divinity which is unlimited Love. In ACIM this is called giving it to the Holy Spirit. In other spiritual traditions this is called Satsang.

Function

In ACIM Jesus says our only function is completion. Completion is the recognition and celebration of Divinity, perfect, whole and complete as it is and to cease the denials that we are already this. This is a different function from the ways of the world that confuses function with roles and responsibilities for achievement, collecting objects and achieving. The question is always, *What is it for? What is the purpose?* Our only function is to express Divine nature in wholeness–all that is given by the Father. There is no other function or purpose. Our sole function in this world is to transcend the idea of limitation of a personal identity. There is no other function for this world. Amen.

Healing

Healing is a helpful thought, the recognition that Divinity is denied and the denials must be looked at through the Light of forgiveness to see the desire to experience thought, feelings, emotions–all the changing appearances that seem to be real and must be recognized as denials of Divine Light. There is neither a healer nor a healed, yet this must be recognized and accepted as truth for lasting peace of mind. Healing is not of the body, all healing takes place in the mind–consciousness, ceasing to accept the fragmentation of consciousness and the experience of lack and limitation. It may–and often does–reflect as what appears to be a healing in the body, yet this is only an expression of change in form, which is not a reflection of Absolute reality, which does not know change. It is merely an opportunity to look beyond form and the miscreation, the desire to experience form as real.

Holy Relationship

Jesus discussions Holy Relationship at length in *A Course in Miracles*. Relationships of the world are a means in which the ego perpetuates itself through the experience that there are others to have a relationship with. Jesus shifts the focus of relationships in the world from attempting to join through bodies, to see where attempting to find love through bodies is a means to deny Divinity, that Love is everything. Brothers become the means that speed spiritual awakening by revealing where Divinity and wholeness is denied. When relationships of the world are given to the Light in guidance to see what is true and cease denials, relationships become holy representatives of the pure relationship that God always has with His holy Son.

Holy Spirit

The Holy Spirit is the Light that lights everyone who is born. The Light of Truth within all beings. This is the Light of intuition that can provide guidance and direction for the fastest means to Spiritual Awakening. The ego attempts to block following intuition, this is a means to attempt to preserve personal identity and thus pain and suffering. The Holy Spirit–and Jesus–is also called the Voice for God. This is the inner voice that provides guidance and intuition that speeds the recognition of Divinity.

Honesty of God

In ANC ACIM Jesus speaks of Honesty of God. Honesty of God is acknowledgement of Divine Light as true reality, admitting the desire to experience denials (pain and suffering) that Light is the only reality, and ceasing to deny that the Light is all that is.

Jesus

Jesus is a helpful concept in the mind of the dreamer. This is the symbol within consciousness of evolution of consciousness back to the natural state of Divinity. It reflects the desire of the dreamer to experience crucifixion and thus pain and suffering through denial of Divinity and the reunification of consciousness to spiritual awakening of the dreamer through resurrection. Jesus represents Christ consciousness and the collapse of the idea of consciousness to Choiceless Awareness–unity with Absolute reality. Jesus is an appearance of superconsiousness, the reminder that consciousness is not unified and thus represents the call for consciousness to cease to deny peace and joy through fragmentation–objective experience–and thereby rest and celebrate Love and natural state of being, being synonymous with Light. Jesus can be considered to be the voice for reason, e.g. non-duality, in a mad, upside down world of duality. It is the voice within that guides the way back to Absolute reality. This voice of wisdom is the same as Higher Self, Holy Spirit, intuitive knowing of God, Guidance and Voice for God. Jesus does not claim to be different nor apart; he is a part of the whole. In ACIM text he suggests that he can be viewed as an older and wiser brother offering guidance. This is helpful until it is seen that Jesus is merely a part of the whole–consciousness–that calls those experiencing fragmentation and suffering back to the recognition and celebration of Unicity.

Judgment

Judgment is the desire to experience duality. To experience judgment requires two–something that can be judged and one who judges. This is immediate experience of duality and thus all pain and suffering. It is a denial of Infinite Light. Since the desire for the experience of more than one miscreates perception, judgment is healed perception through forgiveness, the collapse of the perception of duality.

Listen and Follow, Follow the Light within, Follow the Holy Spirit, Voice for God or Inner Light.

In A Course in Miracles a helpful means is offered to speed spiritual awakening through the recognition of Divine Light and learning to listen to Divine Light–the memory of Divine power which is denied through the investment in the experience of the changing, the ego. To learn to listen and follow is to learn to hear the voice for truth (in ACIM this is called the Holy Spirit), which is the Voice for God–the voice that recognizes original Divine nature. To follow this inner guidance or intuition is the expression of Divinity as it is whole and complete. It is tuning into what is original–the natural state of being What Is. To follow the Voice for God within is to align with Divine nature and to cease to deny Divine nature, which is infinite, unchanging Love. The ego is a denial of the Voice for God within. Following the Light within is a fast means to spiritual awakening as following the Light within is a denial that the ego, the sense of limitation, exists.

Mighty Companions

Mighty companions are not specifically mentioned in this text; however, they are discussed in ACIM text and referred to in Light Circles. Mighty companions refer to those beings that join together for the purposes of recognition of Divine nature–all is One, in contrast to many relationships and friendships that are often used to prove that separation is real. This is joining in holy purpose to see what is true. In some spiritual traditions mighty companions are called Sangha and joining to see what is true is called Satsang.

Mind, Right Mindedness, Wrong Mindedness

In many non dual traditions the term mind is referred to as synonymous with the ego. In ACIM Jesus refers to Infinite Mind as absolute reality. In order to assist with discernment of where Light is denied through the ego he adds two distinctions. Right mindedness, which are thoughts in alignment with the Light, including thoughts of love, unity, God, happiness and joy, and the ACIM Course Lessons. Wrong mindedness is the decision and thus desire to experience pain, suffering and death through the ego that arises out of the belief in separation. This includes all forms of judgment.

Miracle

A miracle is a change in perception. The ego is false perception, the perception of separation from the all that is. Thus a miracle through forgiveness is the undoing of false perception which leads to unified perception of wholeness.

Purpose

Purpose is a means of focusing on Truth of Divine Light rather than the fiction of the world apart from the whole. When Jesus says purpose is our only function, he means our only purpose for this life is the recognition of Divinity and to cease to deny it. To celebrate Divine Life in fullness. Thus our purpose is to transcend personal identity, to transcend the moving and changing–consciousness.

Resurrection

Resurrection is the symbol of spiritual awakening, the unceasing recognition and celebration of Divine nature, as God and the Holy Son of God can never be separate. Time and space is impossible, only unchanging Infinite Love is real. Resurrection is the falling away of the desire to experience death by denying Infinite Light as the only true reality.

Suppression and repression

Light is all there is and the unity of all that is. In order for recognition of Light not to be self apparent, recognition of the Light is suppressed and repressed through the dream of separation, meaning it is held below the level of awareness by dreaming. This is the energy of desire and the associated beliefs that are held in the subconscious mind to deny Light. This is the suppression of peace of mind, joy and love–Self denial–which is the basis for all suffering. In the place of infinite peace of mind power is given to the energies of denial of Divinity; this is miscreation. These energies must be released into the Light–seen as untrue in the Light of truth and thus forgiven–for the Light, the Kingdom of Heaven, to be consistent experience.

The I am, or I am presence

While this book does not refer specifically to the I am presence it is helpful to refer to it here since it is discussed in many spiritual traditions. Beingness is the I am presence in which the original God principle shines into the manifest. The Light–Absolute reality–is the unspeakable silence and is before the I am presence. The I am presence is an expression of consciousness, the Son of God. Some traditions refer to Awareness as synonymous with consciousness. Jesus, like Nasargadatta Maharaj, distinguishes consciousness to be different from the Awareness. While manifest cannot be separated in truth from unmanifest, Infinite Light is beyond manifest and unmanifest. The full expression of the I am presence is the recognition that the manifest and unmanifest are the same, Christ consciousness in expression through a seeming body, yet beyond the idea of a body.

Tiny mad idea, Dream of separation from Source

In ACIM Jesus refers to the tiny mad idea. The tiny mad idea is the idea or thought believed that it is possible to be separate from the Light and that what is changing is real. From this one thought all of consciousness spun out as a dream of change and fragmented into a dream of separation from Source; all suffering comes from the desire for and thus belief in the tiny mad idea. It is impossible to be separate from Source, all that is, and thus the tiny mad idea reflects the insanity of the belief that separation from Source and a different reality from Infinite Light is possible. Since separation from Divine Light is impossible, it must be experienced as a dream. A desired dream of falling asleep and not recognizing Absolute reality and of waking up to Absolute reality. This is the insane idea that the Son of God is separate from the Father–the desire for consciousness–the experience of the changing.

Willingness

Willingness is an expression within consciousness of openness to accept all that it given by the Father. The ego is the expression of consciousness to deny all that is given by the Father. Thus willingness to see things differently in the Light of Truth through forgiveness is to learn the ways of the Holy Spirit–Divine Light. This is the expression of Divinity which is Love, unlimited by concepts of time and space. Willingness is an expression of openness to look outside of the ego thought system that seems real to see the only reality is Divine Light. It is the willingness to see that death is unreal and has no dominion over the Son of God. This is the humility to look with the Light and admit that all denials of Divinity are untrue.

Joining in Light Devotional Center

The Center is a silent monastery where beings move in silence, dedicating their lives to selfless service and devotion to awakening to true nature. The Center is an expression and celebration of unconditional love of the Self, the Light of Infinite Being. It was opened in May 2019 in guidance from Jesus to extend the speed to spiritual awakening offered by *A Course in Miracles* and *Jesus: A New Covenant ACIM.*

The purpose of the Center is to invite everyone to join in Light–the Truth of Love's ever-presence–by extending the non-dual mystical teachings of Jesus through Light Circles, devotional stays for mind training/karma yoga (seva, selfless service to Love) program, retreats, Satsang, and silent contemplation. Occasionally the Center is open for visitors for Satsang, spiritual movies, and silent contemplation on the nature of Infinite Being. We ask visitors to honor the contemplative silence while at the monastery. This means no speaking unless essential and if speaking please whisper quietly with an awareness of those nearby. If you would like more information, please email join@JoininginLight.net.

About Cay Villars

Cay is a mystic in full devotion to following the Voice of Jesus in the continual celebration of inner Light. Some call this Enlightenment or Union with God. She is called the "laughing mystic" for the joy and sense of humor expressed in Satsang/Joining in Light Sessions.

She began hearing a Voice while volunteering as a behavioral change coach in prisons for men and women in Wisconsin. While studying *A Course in Miracles* she experienced mystical visions in which Jesus appeared. In a vision he gave her the blue Joining in Light image, a powerful symbol of the healing power of joining to celebrate the Light within.

Her storyline "in the world" included executive coaching, management, marketing, intuitive healer, and scientist, which led to the realization that there is no storyline of more value than the happiness of Divine Being in celebration of all the Love there is.

Cay teaches that everyone can hear and follow Jesus/the Voice for God as the fastest means to Enlightenment, the complete undoing of the ego to transcend all pain, illness and suffering of the world. This is the joy and peace that surpasses understanding. She is Director for the Joining in Light Silent Devotional Center.

Made in the USA
Coppell, TX
08 May 2022

77558202R00102